T0194818

LISTEN
To The
SILENCE

MESSAGES & MIRACLES FROM
SPENCER WHO NEVER SPOKE WORDS

SPENCER L. GRAY &
GINA G. GRAY

BALBOA.PRESS
A DIVISION OF HAY HOUSE

Balboa Press books may be ordered through booksellers or by contacting:

Balboa Press
A Division of Hay House
1663 Liberty Drive
Bloomington, IN 47403
www.balboapress.com
844-682-1282

Because of the dynamic nature of the Internet, any web addresses or
links contained in this book may have changed since publication and
may no longer be valid. The views expressed in this work are solely those
of the author and do not necessarily reflect the views of the publisher,
and the publisher hereby disclaims any responsibility for them.

The author of this book does not dispense medical advice or prescribe the use
of any technique as a form of treatment for physical, emotional, or medical
problems without the advice of a physician, either directly or indirectly. The
intent of the author is only to offer information of a general nature to help
you in your quest for emotional and spiritual well-being. In the event you use
any of the information in this book for yourself, which is your constitutional
right, the author and the publisher assume no responsibility for your actions.

Any people depicted in stock imagery provided by Getty Images are
models, and such images are being used for illustrative purposes only.
Certain stock imagery © Getty Images.

Print information available on the last page.

ISBN: 979-8-7652-4027-4 (sc)
ISBN: 979-8-7652-4029-8 (hc)
ISBN: 979-8-7652-4028-1 (e)

Library of Congress Control Number: 2023904691

Balboa Press rev. date: 04/03/2023

Spencpiration #1

If you were meant to look back, your head would turn that way.

Spencer's Mayan Spirit animal was an owl. Of course, they can turn their heads around and look back! Spencer's wisdom was never doubted. He now shape-shifts and appears often as an owl to his Madre and his Dad.

CONTENTS

Foreword..ix

Introduction...xiii

Dedication From Spencer...xv

1   What Is Joy?...1

2   Let's Talk about Orbs..11

3   Shifting Shapes...21

4   Miracles and Magic..35

5   Speaking through Songs...47

6   Playing with Numbers..65

7   Seven Silent Years...79

8   The Jasons..91

9   Endings Matter...101

About the Authors...111

FOREWORD

I knew Spencer was wise the moment he was laid on my chest when he was born. When we first connected eye to eye, I heard him clearly tell me we were in for a wild ride together! And oh boy ... we really did live life when he was here. One of Spencer's favorite songs is "Not Every Man Lives" by Jason Aldean. Spencer embraced his life with an attitude of *Here I Am! Alive! Fully empowered to be who I am and to do what I came here to do!* What he came here to do was be who he was—and still is—which is unconditional love.

When Spencer was first born, I didn't know he would never be able to talk or walk. It didn't stop him from being the creator of his own world. He always remembered to use his imagination to get through every day, and he taught everyone he met the power of unconditional love. He accepted all people's "less than perfect" ways and demonstrated joy and strength his entire twenty-three years. His favorite expression that he used as his universal language was his great smile! Spencer was, and still is, pure love, and when in his presence, the essence of love is *felt*.

When Spencer told me this book would be from *his* perspective, I had to rethink everything I had written over the years because I had thought the book would be from *my* perspective as his Madre de la Tierra (Earth Mother)—this is what he started calling me after he dropped his body.

The first issue he clarified was that he had to leave so the book could be written. His leaving was an ending; however, it was also a new beginning of nurturing this relationship that was, is, and always will be. Over the past three years, I have learned about my relationship with several of my Spirits, Guides, and Guards who are *always* with me *in all ways,* as Spencer says!

These relationships have *felt* so beautiful, loving, and nurturing to my Spirit Soul and heart. Of course, losing Spencer nearly destroyed my heart, and the wall I built around it to protect it was stubborn to remove completely. If I hadn't connected with my Spirits, Guides, and Guards, I may have chosen to leave when Spencer did. Since I was fortunate to have shared in his transition journey, I am acutely aware of how beautiful and peaceful it is where he now exists in perfect union with his Spirit Soul. It's hard not to long to be there with him. My time will come …

Spencer had been in frequent communication with me using telepathic messages and song lyrics throughout his final twenty-three days. Within a few hours of his transcendence, he told me what he wanted to share on his social media page to inform people of his passing.

We posted these song titles on the day he transcended: I'm "Blacktop Gone" to "My Kinda Party" and "I'll See You When I See You." We had been listening to Jason Aldean on shuffle for many hours during Spencer's final days, and he knew exactly what he wanted to say about his own exit.

Spencer continues to use music to communicate quite clearly and loudly! He also shape-shifts, speaks directly to me and others, uses the numbers three, nine, and twenty-three, appears in dreams, and loves to dance and play as an orb or two!

This book will share stories with messages and miracles that go far beyond Spencer's passing to his continued expansion into the highly evolved being (HEB) that he is.

This poem was one of the first beautiful messages I received from Spencer shortly after he transcended to True Light.

—Gina Gray, Scribe for Spencer Gray

"Eternal"
Spencer Lloyd Gray

I'm in the air,
    I'm everywhere!
        I'm in the sea—
            Just watch for me!

I'm in the sky;
    You know I can fly!
        I'm in the sand;
            Just feel me in your hand!

I'm in the fire;
    I ride the embers higher and higher!
        I'm in the earth
            Because you gave me birth!

I'm in your heart—
    We are never apart!
        I'm in the light,
            And with you, I will fight!

INTRODUCTION
Gina Gray, Scribe for Spencer

Spencer Lloyd Gray was a very bright Light Being who was born into his earth suit on December 7, 1995. He was my son who lived twenty-three years in his special body before transcending to the True Light on February 8, 2019.

Spencer loved musician Jason Aldean and often used his song lyrics to communicate many messages to his family and friends while he was here in body. When he dropped his body, he gained access to an infinite source of songs, artists, and lyrics and soon began to send me messages through music, poetry, orbs of light, numbers, or simple words every day.

I started writing the messages down and began to call them *"Spencpirations."* These quickly evolved to more vivid form, with inspirational, brilliant ideas and words of unconditional love coming through loud and clear. Spencer had been communicating with me this way throughout his entire life because he never used words to speak. We communicated by sharing thought forms with each other, and I would voice his desire whenever he and I figured out what he wanted.

I began writing this book when Spencer was six years old. I had already learned so much from him about how brilliant he was, even though he didn't speak words. He remains my greatest

Spirit, Guide, Guard, and eternal teacher. I knew this book would be written because the value in nurturing the relationship with silent Spirit beings is much greater than a physical connection as Mama and son.

The greatest lesson Spencer taught me was to learn to **Listen to the Silence**. This has enabled me to continue to communicate with him.

I did learn, and this book is the Eternal Life Story of one powerful Spirit being named **Spencer Lloyd Gray**. After he transcended to the True Light, he soon let me know that this book was to be written from *his* point of view, not mine. I am forever grateful to have been chosen to share this journey with Spencer as his Madre de la Tierra (Earth Mother) and beyond.

—Gina Gayle Gray
Grapevine, Texas
Nuevo Vallarta, Mexico
www.listentothesilence.org
www.anywheremindbodysoul.com

DEDICATION FROM SPENCER

I WANT TO DEDICATE THIS BOOK TO ALL NON-VERBAL communicators and the people who cross paths with them. May the speaking people learn to "listen to the silence" of the others so we can all expand together into the infinite and eternal space where acceptance thrives and judgement dissolves.

I am *eternally grateful* for all those who crossed my earthbound path for moments, hours, days, weeks, months, years, lifetime, or many lifetimes. Every life matters!

My Dad and my Mama were my partners I chose well. My Dad always included me in all his fun activities with his friends my entire life. I enjoyed every minute we spent together and continue to do so now! I am with you both ALWAYS and IN ALL WAYS.

1

WHAT IS JOY?

AS YOU MAY KNOW, JOY IS ONE OF THE MOST ELUSIVE EMOTIONS—
and one of the most important to remember how to *feel*! When
you experience joy, the *feeling* is one of the highest vibratory states
to be enjoyed in human form and beyond. It can be *felt* when you
are in the essence of pure unconditional love, and when you are
in the presence of someone you are in love with.

Love is a place. When you're there, you know it. You know
it because you *feel* the wave of joy within and beyond your entire
being. It is a knowing. When you *fly to love*—which can be done
anytime from anywhere—and you arrive, you know it, you *feel*
it, and you become it.

I've used my smile to express my gift of joy throughout my
life. Since I didn't have access to spoken words, I found a smile to
be readily available and free to share anytime. During my twenty-
three years in body, I crossed paths with many people who had
lost their connection to their joy. I spent my life in observation
mode because the body I was given for my existence as Spencer
wasn't able to do much without assistance. I was usually in the
middle of things wherever people in my life were congregating.
I watched people, listened to them, and gave the only thing I had

to give to everyone I met—my unconditional love expressed on the wave of joy.

Joy is worth remembering because it is a lightness that you *feel* that reminds you that you are able to *fly to love* anytime you choose. This is where I am at home. Joy is the wave that you ride into and out of the **place called love.**

Love is a place where all Spirit Souls are at home. Human beings spend their entire lifetimes flying to and from love without ever realizing or remembering this.

Joy isn't something you can hold in your hand. It's the thing you *feel* when you hold the hand of another. It's meant to lift you to a place of higher vibratory frequency so you can enjoy the *experience of joy.* This can be fleeting but is also sustaining. You remember what this *feels* like when you are reminded by the emotions you experience when you see a beautiful sunrise, sunset, or moonrise over the horizon, when you laugh with someone in joyous happiness, or when you *feel* unconditional love and gratitude for your family, like I did for my Mama, my Dad, and my sister, Alexis.

Joy *feels* like freedom and connection at the same time. When you realize or remember that we are all unique, sovereign beings (freedom) who are connected to one another in some part of our existence (connection), it's important to *feel* that symbiotic nature of this relationship. This is **connected freedom.** Keeping this in harmony is important. The wave—or joy—is the flow of your unseen self, moving from **the place called love** to your earth body, in and out every day and night! While you're in love during your waking life or your sleep, you bathe in the essence of love and then are coated in those qualities as you return to your physical body on earth. That beautiful essence is then readily available to share naturally with others. This is how to share love and joy with each other! It's simple, although not easy.

Take time each day to pause. This is what **Listen to the Silence** is really about. When you tune in to your inner guidance, which is your own best specialist living inside you, you know things! You can trust that this wisdom comes through in messages and miracles whispered by your own Spirits, Guides, and Guards who are with your Spirit Soul *always* and *in all ways*.

Joy is meant to be shared, which is why it's so contagious. When humor and comedy are evoking the emotion of happiness, laughter is the result. When you hear another person laughing, you catch the wave of that emotion because it is expressing joy. The flow of that *feeling* is worth integrating into your life every day. Find places to go every day where you can hear the laughter of happiness: Children playing in a park; families enjoying a day at the beach; the giggling of vibrant teenage girls dancing their way through life as they dream about finding their first romantic encounter; or watching videos of hilarious antics of cats and dogs are sure to lift your vibration.

I loved using music to help bring joy into all daily activities throughout my earth life. I began using the lyrics of songs to "talk" to my family and friends when I was quite young. Whenever I was stuck expressing my wants and needs, I would hear a line in a song that said the exact words I needed to piece together a message that I knew would be understood. My lovely attendant, Jessica, and I would listen to music and make playlists to use for me to choose words and sentences for my own use in communicating with others. This was the beginning of my enhanced telepathic messaging abilities, and I had twenty-three years in a body that didn't speak words to polish my gift!

The experience of joy is to be shared. This is why the value of being together with others is such an important component of joy. I was fortunate to live my life in a home where celebrations were common occurrences. We had large gatherings for birthdays, Thanksgiving, Christmas, New Year's, Independence Day, bonfires, and full moons! Any reason was a good excuse to get together with friends and family to share in joy. The houses we lived in were large, and having guests over for days, weeks, or months was an ongoing theme. Our guests were always well accommodated, and great times were had by all.

The best time every year was the Christmas season. The joy that comes along with that time is nearly impossible to miss! My birthday was December 7, so I never wanted to see the Christmas season start until after the celebration of my own birth. But starting December 8, the lights started going up throughout the house. I insisted that every banister and most windows be well lit. And it was so. Every year we had three decorated trees inside the house, as well as lights on trees outside. The main tree every year was fourteen feet tall and covered in the most beautiful decorations and lights.

The presents underneath the tree were endless, and the beauty of the wrapping paper being reflected by the lights on the tree was such a brilliant sight to behold. I loved to lie under the tree looking up and out above the lights on the tree, above the star, beyond the room, the house, the earth, into that infinite, eternal time-space where there is no time or space. There just *is*.

The true story of Christmas is displayed in the cosmos when our sun reaches the top of its cycle on December 25, shortly after the winter solstice. Every year at this time, it lines up with the star Sirius, who gives new life (birth) to our sun. This is the *original* story of Christmas laid out beautifully in the stars in the sky. I knew how to astral travel, so when I was very few earth years old, I would use these opportunities with our Christmas tree to pop out for some extra joy.

My Mama knew about this also, and we shared many astral travel journeys when I was still there. We would soar together through the skies while lying on a beach or on a boat somewhere or sitting by the firepit in our backyard. We also spent many nights in communion with Lady Luna, which is why I still appear to Madre de la Tierra as an orb whenever she goes out on the beach for some moonrise experiences.

During a recent full moon in Puerto Morelos, Mexico, I danced up the moonlit path reflected on the water, then hovered above it before flying up the beach to sit with her. She has photos and videos of many full moons we shared after I left. In the videos, I can be seen as an orb dancing around the moon and darting about to other lights in the sky, such as Jupiter or Altair. She has videos of me moving along the moonlight to come close to her where she's sitting on the beach. I showed off for her and my sister, Alexis, in Sedona, Arizona, when they watched the moonrise over the mountains at the Airport Mesa Vortex there. We've experienced several moments of **connected freedom** under the light of Lady Luna since I left.

This brings immense joy to each of us every time we get to watch a moonrise together! We share in this *feeling,* and that happiness expressed as joy radiates out to reach others. What a beautiful cycle to repeat! I was always happy when I was able to experience many moonlit skies with my Dad and my Mama during my twenty-three years on earth. And now we each know that we are still connected to each other through La Luna—and other lights in the night sky—as she reflects back to us every emotion we *felt* or need to *feel* in order to continue to work toward infinite and eternal freedom and connection. This is **connected freedom** at its best.

Joy is in the stars that shine brightly in the night sky. I know because this is where I am now. Many of these lights are portals to other places, infinite and eternal places, such as **the place called love**.

Many stars are gateways into other worlds in the light realm universes, and some lead into complete darkness in the dark realm universes. Both energies are necessary. One is not good and the other bad. They are not opposing forces. Dark and light are to be blended, swirled, merged, expanded, and integrated rather than experienced as separate. When you remember how to play with this, you will *feel* the **connected freedom** to all that

I'm talking about. Joy is the wave that moves between it all, and that's where you can find me now. I am freedom and connection. I am **connected freedom**, and I now use this to communicate with Madre de la Tierra and others in many magical ways.

I can use a combination of methods to get my messages through. This I do often. I took the opportunity one night in June 2020 to draw my Madre's attention to a star named Altair, which is one of the stars in the Summer Triangle. Once I knew she was "locked on" to Altair, I invited her for an astral travel meeting, which she accepted.

We met in the starlight and played joyously for a beautiful moment. When it was time for Madre to return home to her earth body, I *felt* her hesitancy and assured her that I was always nearby. We agreed we would meet again soon, and we did. The next night we met again and had a lovely dance in the starlight. By this time, Madre had used her sky guide to identify the star I was coming from as Altair.

A few days later I found another way to communicate with my Madre about this important star. She was in search of some new piano music to inspire her for a writing assignment she was working on. I took the opportunity to use music to send her a message, and it worked brilliantly. She was listening to some new piano music she had found (following my guidance) by David Lanz, and the words she wrote flowed effortlessly on to the keyboard. Then another song began, and she stopped her writing immediately while she gave the song her full attention as she listened to the music. She *felt* the music dancing on her heart strings. The artist was playing the piano, but there were no lyrics, only the title of the song. Madre was stunned when she read the title that touched her deeply. It is called "Wings to Altair."

Words were not necessary for me to convey this message to my Madre. The name of the star, the journey we took flying to Altair a few nights earlier, combined with the piano music swept her away and up into a higher frequency where she can hear and *feel* my messages of joy. I told her that anytime she hears "Wings to Altair," she can be certain that I will appear for a visit. We have used this to celebrate together many times since then. I also asked her to share this song and my promise to appear with a few other people. I will continue to add people to this list when they're ready.

I do know something about losing your connection to your joy. When I was in the hospital in 2012 with RSV (respiratory syncytial virus), I actually left for the True Light one night. My contract was up, and it was time for me to leave. As my Spirit Soul was soaring above my body, I saw my Dad holding me and my Mama out in the hall screaming for help. I had "coded" and was already gone, but I looked back and saw their intense pain, shock, fear, and heartbreak, and I *felt* their immense love for me. My Mama's Soul was wailing and my Dad was frozen in time-space, unable to function. I *felt* I had to go back to spend more time with these people who had given so much of their lives to celebrate and honor me. In that moment, I agreed to sign an addendum to my Soul Contract and added another seven years.

The new conditions were rough. I was now dependent upon a ventilator to keep me alive. I couldn't breathe on my own so had a tracheostomy for the last years of my life. I became a medical patient but refused to give up or give in to medicine to keep me alive. I needed my cuff on my trach tube to always be inflated for my own comfort, so I could no longer make any sound or smell or taste food. This was a painful realization that came slowly over time while I recovered from RSV, and I did not take it well as my new limitations were revealed. I had reached the end of my patience with my physical existence and knew then that my final years would be lived without the wave of joy that had been my expression my entire life up to that point. I'm not saying I didn't have a great deal of enjoyment in my final seven years, but the *true joy* that I had known so well the first sixteen years was left waiting for me in the star, Altair, from the night I coded. I was reunited with *true joy* when I transformed into my Spirit Soul on February 8, 2019.

Keep joy in your life! Share joy with others every chance you get. Learn from cultures that do this, like the Mexicans where my Madre de la Tierra—Earth Mother—lives. The local families occupy the beach on Sundays and express pure joy the entire day. They live in joy most days, and this closeness is something my Dad enjoys with his friends, who all support him faithfully.

You cannot have joy in your life, in your Soul, and not want to share it with others. Seek joy, receive joy, give joy, share joy, *be* joy! Go for this highest vibratory frequency that you can use to soar to **the place called love** whenever you want. Do this often to remember that the essence of love is what you were, are, and always will be, and joy is the emotion you deserve to experience most often throughout your earth days, months, or years. Be the joy. Be the essence of love that we are all born to be.

My Madre wrote this poem when I was in the hospital having my first hip osteotomy surgery in 2002. It expresses our unspoken telepathic communication abilities quite well because as I was recovering from the procedure, she was writing this, and I was sharing the experience together with her. These were rehearsals for how we would continue to play together after I dropped my body.

"Spencer's Smile"
Gina Gayle Gray

I take a ride on his smile anytime
I need to leave this place!
It sweeps me away up out of myself
And into his world of joy beyond his face.

I take a ride on his smile to visit a place
that most won't see until our lives end!

It's only a glimpse on a split-second ride,
And then its beauty and wonder dissolve like the wind.

I take a ride on his smile to see where he goes
to get all his joy!
He carries me there, and I stand at the edge as he jumps
in the pool, waving me in to share his great toy.

I take a ride on his smile.
The tickets are free!
It's always open—
And not just for me.

I take a ride on his smile, and although I must
come right back to my physical life,
I know I'm free to get right back in line.
With one look in his face, I escape all my strife!

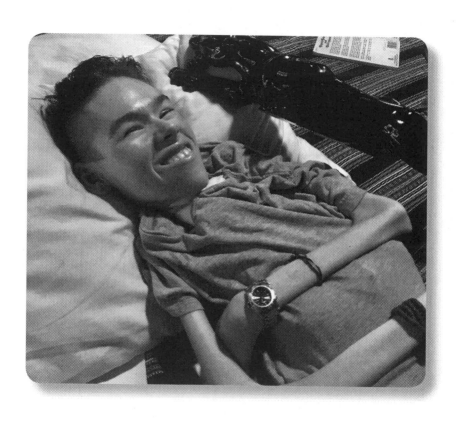

2

LET'S TALK ABOUT ORBS

ARE YOU AWARE OF HOW EASY AND FUN IT IS FOR ME TO APPEAR in your earth realm "peeking" through the veil using orbs? I have now enhanced and expanded my use of light frequencies and was recently able to manifest two orbs to peek through the bedroom window during the early morning hours, while running the lyrics "sometimes I feel like somebody's watching me" sung by Michael Jackson in the song by Rockwell, "Somebody's Watching Me" through my Madre's mind. I did this as my buenos dias message to her on February 8, 2022—the three-year anniversary of my transcendence into my Spirit Soul. The message was well received, and as she attuned to the song, I added, *I've always got your back!* (The window I was peeking through was behind her at the time I appeared!) I also told her that I wanted to see *not* crying for me or the memory of me on that day. She and Alexis, who was visiting her in Puerto Morelos, were directed to go have fun to celebrate life that day if they truly wanted to honor my memory.

I have always been attracted to lights and can easily use this frequency to communicate through the veil from my side to yours. I first appeared as two orbs in the TV screen at our home at 329 Country Court to let my Madre know that I approved of

a L* head

her decision to put our house up for sale. It was time to move on, and I assured her I would send the perfect new owners soon. I also told her she would *know* who they were as soon as she met them. Both Mama and Dad saw me and knew it was me sending them love and light through the dark TV screen at 2:00 a.m. I really enjoy playing around as an orb, or two orbs, whenever either of them take a photo.

I showed up as an orb in a photo of my Madre and uncle Casey taken at my first birthday party after I dropped my body. I can clearly be seen in the photo "sitting" directly over my Madre's right shoulder. It was seen by everyone at my party, and they all knew I was right there with them, enjoying the special way they celebrated by birthday! I also show up in photos my Dad takes when he's out in nature or on a lake or watching a sunset or moonrise. I've even perfected my ability to illuminate myself during daylight hours. I can be seen in beautiful sunrise photos as an orange-colored orb at the water's edge where the sunlight touches the beach.

I was always fascinated by lights and wanted to see as many as possible, whether on a truck, trailer, or the Christmas tree. The energy is exactly what I need to shine my inner light brightly. When I was in my earth body, I was attracted to all the shiny metals as well. Copper was my favorite, and I loved gold, silver, and chrome too. I also enjoyed a strong connection to many precious stones, and after I left, I used their energy to communicate with Madre. I sent her an ad for *The Book of Stones*, and at first she was resistant to buying it. But I kept reminding her, so she ordered it. When it arrived, I had her let me guide it open, and I took her to a special stone called Auralite 23. When she read about its qualities, she nearly fell to the floor because the energy of this stone is quite similar to mine when I was in body. I wanted to connect with her using this special stone, and the energy it emits is magical. The number twenty-three is an important factor in the name of this stone, and I'll talk about it more in a later chapter. I use it often to send messages.

When I was a baby, my favorite toy to play with when I stayed at my sweet neighbor Joan's house was a car dashboard. Everything on the toy lit up or made noise. When it stopped working, Joan would make the sounds so we could continue to play with the toy.

When Joan became very ill and transcended physical life, she soon visited me using the power of her Spirit Soul. I was playing with my car dashboard on the floor at my house and suddenly it lit up! Madre turned the toy over and the battery cover was off—no batteries at all! We immediately knew it was Joan lighting the toy. I later used this skill I learned from Joan and played with my aunt Vicki, who was packing up my collection of Hess trucks. She was removing all their batteries and putting them in their boxes to be passed on to others. I took the opportunity to light up one of my favorite firetrucks *after* Vicki had removed the batteries. She was so tuned in to my presence that she laughed joyously and immediately found my Madre to share the story with her.

Joan reminded me how to make myself visible as an orb very early in my newly transcended Spirit Soul body. She was one of my first loving guides to greet me after I transcended—not during my process. Our Souls were previously connected through our earth-body relationship, and I enjoyed reuniting with her in **the place called love.**

Ten days before I transcended, my Madre and I were lying in bed together, and we shared a very clear vision of Joan and several other neighbors who had crossed over. They were gathered in Spirit form outside our back door, and when my Madre asked Joan why they were there, she answered, "We're here to watch Spencer transcend." We understood that they were lining my pathway supporting me but were not my destination. This was clear to my Spirit Soul. In this vision, the neighbors were all in a group along the right side of my path.

Then we noticed another brilliant Light Being up and to the left. This was a majestic, powerful presence, and we both knew immediately that it was my Grandpa Jack, who was Madre's Dad. We knew he was the True Light, and a Watcher, and that I would see him when I dropped my body. Grandpa Jack had been in contact with me since he passed suddenly on Christmas Day 1999. I was only four at that time, and his Spirit Soul stayed very close, watching over me and my Madre after he left. He is an extension of the Archangel Michael, a Watcher collective, and his presence was powerful. I knew I could trust his guidance completely to lead me into the True Light for my transcendence process.

Grandpa Jack had used dashboard lights to get my Madre's attention many times after he left. He would flash the brake light on the dashboard in multiple vehicles she drove after he left. His message for my Madre was to *slow down* in life and seek more enjoyment. It was powerful, and once she finally acknowledged that she understood, she received many more messages from him over the years.

He has been my companion, my guide and teacher in this area of my new role without a body. We enjoy spending time together now working for humanity as light warriors in Watcher angel collective form. He is part of the collective representing the sacred masculine aspect of every Spirit Soul, as am I. (I will share about this collective of Watchers that is named The Jasons in a later chapter.)

I also work together with several divine feminine Spirit aspects that include my aunt Nancy, my aunt Susie, my Mimi and her sister Ethel, my neighbors Evelyn and Nancy, and my grandmas Ethel and Mabel, who are also beautiful beings of True Light here where I am in **the place called love**. I have learned about the use of light to expand beyond the shape of an orb to be seen as other creative colors (hues), levels of brightness, or designs (sacred geometry) and can now blend sound with light easily to enhance message delivery. Sound is light slowed down. I have returned to my true highest self, my Spirit Soul, which every human is. Humans ("hue"mans) are light manifested into form, and when we drop our physical bodies, we return to our Light bodies, which are eternal and infinite. Light and sound are unified in the cosmos, as are dark and light. *The place called love* is where these constructs are cleansed and clarified so they can be reintegrated within every Spirit Soul that makes their way back to this realm. Joy is the frequency wave that one must catch and surrender into if they desire this experience in and of the essence of love.

There's a Divine Light Being whose name is Shima. She is who appeared to guide me when my Spirit Soul was ready to leave. She is beautiful and gentle and tender. Going with her into the gold and silver swirling light she embodies was *felt* as pure *ecstasy*! It's interesting to mention that, according to my "invisible garment" (which I wore when I was Spencer Gray), it is a construct presented by Connie Kaplan in her book called "The Invisible Garment", my Soul Purpose during my lifetime was *ecstasy*.

Shima has been my constant companion since I've been without my physical body. I am always in joy and ecstasy because I'm always with Shima. She is bathed in a beautiful gold and silver light that is the essence of *the place called love*. Shima introduced herself to my Madre on 2/2/2020, six days before the one-year anniversary of my transcendence.

While she was in the bathtub that night, Madre heard, "Everything can be transformed into Light."

She sat up in the tub and asked, "What did you say?"

The message was repeated. So Madre got out of the tub and took her journal and began a conversation with the messenger she would later learn was Shima.

She asked, "What do I call you?"

The answer was, "Shima." The message was given: "Many things will be revealed soon about Spencer's transition into the True Light, and the entire process will be known."

My Madre was being told that she would play an important role in the future helping others transition into the True Light, and she would also be guided through a journey to learn how to help others—especially other Mothers who have lost their children—to reconnect with the Spirit Souls of their children within their hearts.

A few days after this message was received, more came through to her and she wrote them down. And then one day, as Madre was meditating, she put her music on shuffle and began her meditation process. Soon into it, she hears the words, "Shima, Shima, Shima, Shima, Shima, Shima, Shi-ma-ya," being sung. Singer Deva Premal was chanting the name Shima, so once again, music was used to secure the delivery of an important message to my Madre. She knew Shima and her connection to this divine being of True Light was real.

This relationship has evolved and expanded in **grateful connection** to each other and all things emanating from original Source. Now Shima and I teach or *remind* Madre great knowledge and wisdom *always* and *in all ways* use unconditional love and light messages, which she accesses and then shares with others in the fashion of an oracle.

The power of this was demonstrated clearly in November 2020. My Mimi, Dad's Mama, was in her transition process, and Shima and I were there to guide her Spirit Soul into the True Light. Dad was with her at her bedside in her home in the Woodlands, holding her hand and sharing unconditional love with her.

My Madre was at her home in Grapevine listening to her David Lanz piano music on shuffle awaiting a visit from me. I played "Wings to Altair," and as always, she listened carefully to my message. I told her that Shima and I were there for Mimi and asked her to tell my Dad, which she did. She sent the Deva Premal chant song "Shima" to him and asked him to play it softly so he and Mimi could receive the gentle peace, light, and love that was there to escort her Spirit Soul into the True Light. Within a few minutes, Mimi came with us.

Being an oracle only takes one quality: you must be able to discern thinking you know something, *feeling* you know something, and *knowing* you know.

Everyone who is having a human (hue-manifestation) experience at this time *know* things deep within themselves. There is a well within you where eternal and infinite wisdom and knowledge flow freely for anyone to access. To find your way back to this, you must be able to go within and **Listen to the Silence**. What you will hear when you really tune in to this higher vibratory level of being is messages and miracles from your Spirit Soul and several of your own Spirits, Guides, and Guards, who are part of your team. Learning to do this is simple, but not easy. My Madre now offers Freedom Coaching to people who want to remember how to connect to your own Spirit Soul. She supports people in her forty-day Journey Back To Me program to focus on their own self-awareness and needs thirty minutes a day for forty days.

Recently, the immense power of the essence of love was illuminated by the spirit of Venus, also known as the Morning Star, in the pre-sunrise sky to my Madre. There are many Light Beings who express themselves in an infinite number of ways. The bright lights seen in the dark night sky and the pre-sunrise sky are powerful messengers.

My Madre was preparing to enjoy a sunrise on the beach and noticed Venus center stage in the pre-dawn sky. She decided to "Venus gaze" while waiting for the sun to rise. When she did, Venus sent this message very clearly: "I see you. I hear you. I *feel* you. I *know* you."

When every human—manifested light being—remembers their immense creative power and finds their way back to self-love by catching a ride on the wave of joy, they'll be on the path to their *true highest self*. There are multitudes of Light Beings all around every person ready to assist with all things. This team is underutilized by most of you. I want everyone to know how badly all the Light Beings want to be invited into your life. We are your Spirits, Guides, and Guards, and we're here to guide you *always* and *in all ways,* expressing ourselves freely on the wave of joy!

Spencpiration #2

If only you could love yourself the way that I love you!

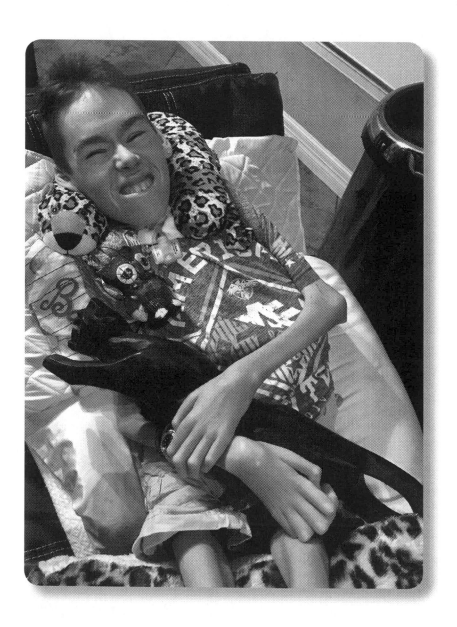

3

SHIFTING SHAPES

My favorite animal is the jaguar, and it is one of the most exhilarating to take on during a shape-shifting adventure. I had a special connection to two jaguars when I was in my earth body. One was named Junior Buddy, and the other was Lucky Boy, who was black. Both jaguars transcended to their Spirit Souls within a few months of my doing so. We were introduced to each other at the Belize Zoo by its founder, Ms. Sharon Matola, who has also recently transcended into her Spirit Soul. Every time I went to her zoo, she took me on a private tour to see *all* the jaguars. She would call them by name, and they would appear as if they were her housecats. Their mutual love for each other was obvious.

I would enjoy being able to show up as a jaguar now to visit my favorite humans, but it isn't likely I will find my people anywhere that jaguars hang out. So, I opted for a "*felt* but not seen" jaguar visit to my Madre one day during summer 2020. She was lying in the backyard beside the pool and was sleeping on my lounger.

I decided to shape shift as Lucky Boy and give her a visit in her dream state. I lightly brushed against her side as I passed by, as cats often do, and she felt me in her sleep state and ran her hand down my back and tail. In her dream she thought she was petting our barn cat, Baggy. But as she began to wake up, she realized it couldn't be him because the height where her hand was stroking was three feet off the ground!

She then took a moment to **Listen to the Silence** and heard me say, "Hello, Mama! I love you! I'm here for a quick visit to remind you that I am now Lucky Boy."

This kind of shape shifting is very simple to do because both Lucky Boy and I are together on *this* side of the veil. It's different when shape shifting using an animal or person that is incarnated and still in the earth suit. In order to do this, an agreement must be secured before popping into another being's body (when following interdimensional code, which I always do).

This is simple with animals because they don't have overdeveloped thinking minds. They're quick to agree because they remember it's all part of the grand adventure of life. I prefer to shape shift as an owl most often. I can find one everywhere, and they are wise animals who understand clearly why I want to "borrow their body" for a visit with some of my favorite humans.

I started borrowing the owls at our home soon after I dropped my body. When I was still in body, we would often hear the barn owls outside my bedroom window around two in the morning— which happened to be the time of my birth into my earth body. Madre and I would lie still and listen to them for several minutes.

I had a deep connection with owl Spirit, as they are my totem Spirit animal, which many indigenous civilizations' belief systems, including Mayan, follow. I knew if I appeared as an owl while this memory was still fresh. Mama and Dad would always recognize me. They both did, so I use this form often, appearing as an owl in one of our trees; or in the trees anywhere my Dad goes in nature; or on the ocean or a lake; or in a painting; or in a book or magazine; or in my Dad's friend Ross's garage; or on the porch at the townhouse I found for a new home after ours was sold; or a tattoo on the leg of a neighbor; or in the jungle in

Puerto Morelos, Mexico; or posted on top of the buildings in El Tigre where my Madre now lives in Vallarta, Mexico.

I have mastered—in partnership with owl Spirit—becoming an owl to have visits with my Mama and my Dad and others since I dropped my body.

Recently, my Madre became sad when she went to bed because she was remembering she and I always playing games on her iPad at bedtime. The moment she dropped into her sadness, I said to her, I'm here with you *always* and *in all ways,* Madre. You *know* this! That got her attention. Then I showed up outside her window, for the first time since she arrived in Mexico, as an owl. She immediately came to the window, and I invited her to come bilocate and sit with me on the branch where I was in the trees in the mangrove behind her house.

We had a lovely Spirit dance together, which is possible for all people to do with their own Spirits, Guides, and Guards. If you have a Spirit that you know well who is on the other side of the veil, you can have a visit with them now easier than when they were here in physical form! Please trust this. When you discover how to release yourself from your physical body on occasion, you will experience the freedom that you were created to live. The remembrance that you are connected to your own physical body and to other human beings is an important aspect of this idea of being in **connected freedom**. These are both worthwhile emotions to experience while you are living your life.

I learned to free myself from my physicality often while I was here for twenty-three years in my body that couldn't move itself and couldn't speak words. Using my imagination, I would go into a *light sleep* stage, where I would leave my physical body to go explore other realms. My attendants thought I was merely taking a nap, but my Madre knew what I was doing. She would call me out on it when she'd come into the room to check on me and find me "napping." I would attempt to get her to come "nap" with me, and we would have a private joke and laugh about it.

When I dropped my body, it was a wonderful *feeling* because my earth body had always been extremely uncomfortable and weak and had become painful my last twenty-three days. I was injured by vaccine injections when I was four months old. My body stopped developing "normally" at that time, and my Madre was painfully aware of this but could not get any supportive response out of the pediatrician when she first noticed and expressed her concerns. When I was nine months old and still could not move my body independently, the doctor agreed to look into things. One trip to the hospital for a brain scan and one negative interpretation by a so-called medical professional, a neurologist, resulted in a diagnosis with a gloomy prognosis.

My Madre and I didn't accept this. We considered the diagnosis to be nothing more than a label that didn't stick, and we sure didn't want any of what they were selling. The "medical mystery" that I became during my twenty-three years baffled the conventional doctors, nurses, therapists, and teachers because I never fit into any of their limited belief systems.

No one could understand how I stayed so healthy and alive without illness in the body I was in. When my Madre asked them why they never used me for their research at Cook Children's Hospital, she was told that I was too healthy! This was when I was in their facility suffering RSV in 2012—and they didn't believe I would ever leave alive. We showed them! My life, including how I chose to live it and how it would end were my choice, and I'm forever grateful that my Madre and Dad **Listened to the Silence** and heard my requests for how I wanted everything handled during my final twenty-three days. I left according to my will and did it *my* way, as everyone should.

The ability to shape shift is a special gift. People who live in physical bodies that are limited in their ability to move about in the 3D realm may learn to activate this talent. This helps endure the minutes, hours, days, nights, weeks, months, and years that pass while being connected to a body that cannot move independently, like I was. You will never hear me complain about my physical situation while I was in my earth body. I was well attended to and never had to worry about whether someone would be around to take care of my needs. I was treated like a king. Can you imagine, even for a minute, being in a body that you had no control over?

The experience gave me great insight into my energetic being. I was always supported physically, emotionally, mentally, spiritually, and energetically by my earth parents, family, and attendants throughout my life. I chose my team carefully, and my people were good people who really cared about being with me. I know most of them realized they weren't around only to *do* things for me. They were there to learn things *from* me. Those who were honest with themselves figured this out soon.

Shape shifting ranges in difficulty and begins simply as borrowing energetic bodies for a short spiritual experience from another energetic being who is on the same side of the veil as I am.

The next level is to borrow the physical body of a being that is in a different form on the earth side of the veil. As I said earlier, using the body of an animal is always much simpler than using another human one. There is so much mental clutter that stops you from enjoying your life! After I transcended to Light, my Dad took a long time to open up to all the possibilities that are now available for us to have experiences together. Of course, his grieving process was deep and very painful for him to bear. So I waited patiently for him to learn to function in a way where light and the essence of love could inspire him to stop looking back and begin moving forward. I sent him messages through songs many times, appeared as an orb or orbs, and shape shifted into an owl, a frog, or a dolphin on multiple visits. I helped him find things he thought he had lost, and popped a photo of myself on his phone to say hello from this side of the veil.

I took an opportunity in November 2019 to master shape shifting and appeared to my Dad in the body of a young man who "magically" showed up at the campsite to help him clean several wild hogs that had been killed on the property that day. Dad was extremely impressed with "my skill level" helping him, and when we were finished with the work, he thanked me and then asked me my name.

I turned to him and said, "My name is Spencer."

He looked into the young man's eyes and *knew* it was me!

Never stop believing … because *believing is seeing.*

I managed to create a second opportunity to meet my Dad while borrowing the body of another young man named Spencer within a few weeks of the first encounter. This time I was wearing round, wire-framed glasses like the ones I wore when I was quite young. The joy that showing up like this for a brief yet powerful visit from my Spirit Soul to yours is immeasurable in my world.

I love to use birds to visit my Madre in Mexico. I've used eagles, owls, ravens, and seagulls on different occasions. She was having lunch on the beach one day and had attracted a few gulls, who were bothering her while she tried to eat. She kept telling them to go away, but one became aggressive toward her, so I decided to swoop in to save the day. I borrowed the body of another gull and flew in between my Madre and the obnoxious bird and told him clearly to leave her alone. He complied and left, along with the other ones who were begging as well. My work was complete, and I flew off to the right alone, back toward where I had borrowed the body and wings of this gull.

My Madre immediately turned toward me as I flew away and shouted, "Thank you, Spencer!"

This knowing that we share that we are now together *always* and *in all ways* is such a beautiful *feeling*! We are capable of astral travel as often as we want and can meet anywhere at any time for a spiritual dance in love. Remember, **love is a place**!

There are so many ways that I can visit my favorite humans now. I'm enjoying my Spirit Soul freedom and being able to explore—in cooperation with many animals—in different ways to communicate messages and miracles. The time is now to step into your Soul suits and remember that being a human is an assignment that everyone agrees to take.

It's also a time to remember that you are all infinite and eternal Spirit Souls who are living a life so you can deliver your unique gifts of service to humanity. Before you can do this, most of you will discover your *physical life purpose* and will experience a way to support yourself that you believe answers the question, "What am I here in this body to *do*?"

Discovering your true highest self while living your life may seem like an impossible task, but I can assure you that the answer to this complicated issue is quite simple. Begin the search now for your *Soul purpose* which is different from your *life purpose*. When you remember what your Soul purpose is and reunite with your Spirit Soul, you'll be able to answer the question, "What am I here in this body with this Soul to *be*?"

Raise your voltage often by opening your emotional receptor sites fully. When you do this, you're tuned to the frequency of your Spirits, Guides, and Guards and will be able to *feel* 360 emotions that are being sent to you every day! Awaken to these *feelings* because emotions are the messengers used by original Spirit Source to communicate with you *always* and *in all ways*. *Feel* the vibration of elation and seek the highest you can every moment!

Once I dropped my physical body and transcended to reconnect with my Spirit Soul, which is eternal and infinite, I soon remembered that I was able to express myself as **connected freedom** in many ways—and I did!

I'm not limited to or bound by any single form but can use a multitude of elements available to me to appear to those who are watching for me. I have shown up as an eagle, a jaguar, an owl, a dolphin, a frog, a raven, a gull, and a moth in physical form to many of my people, who I visit often. I have also shown myself to my Madre using various lights in the night sky as single stars— Altair, Arcturus, Vega, Spica, and Sirius. And I've led her into

27

cosmic knowledge using coded messages I send to her by drawing her attention to a specific constellation.

The first time I communicated to her through the star Altair, she joined me for a dance within the column of light that leads into this special portal. She could not enter because the spinning vortex is too much for human form, but she was able to see and *feel* telepathically what is on the other side. After a few visits to this star, she learned that it is part of a constellation called Aquilla— the Eagle.

I use eagles to deliver messages in many ways to those who are keen enough to listen. Eagles are aware of their surroundings, always watching around and beneath them while soaring in the sky to see life from a higher perspective. I am capable of expressing myself through the eagle in the night sky, using the star Altair, to show myself to my Madre wherever she chooses to lay her head. I've proven this over and over to her since I returned to my Spirit Soul, and she always finds me in the night sky. I use my presence in the Eagle constellation to keep an eye on her everywhere she lives now. Her address in Texas is on Eagle Circle, and I am directly above her home now in Vallarta, Mexico. From her bed at night she sees me watching over her from Altair.

When you activate your imagination, you easily remember that nothing is beyond the reach of your potential! I have given my Madre visions of my adventures in flight taking on the form of unique creations of my making, such as a half jaguar, half eagle. I can take flight as an owl and then morph into an eagle and soar high until I disappear into the sun, needing no form of any kind.

When Madre lived in Puerto Morelos, Mexico, I became creative and decided to visit her as a special messenger. My earth birthday was approaching, and I wanted to assure her that I was with her *always* and *in all ways*. I cocreated this shape-shifting adventure in union with divine feminine Shima, and we appeared as an "IO Moth." She was a beautiful copper red color in the shape of a pyramid. We "magically" appeared one night on Madre's kitchen wall while she was working on her computer at the table. When Madre went to bed later that night, we came into the net around her bed through an opening on the other side from where she slept. She was surprised to see the moth inside the net but was happy to have company for the night. For three days and nights the moth followed her from room to room and back into the net at bedtime. On night three, Madre thought the moth should be set free, but when she tried to leave her on the shrubs outside, she crawled back onto her hand, so Madre brought her back inside. She got back into the net in bed with the moth on her hand, and as she was wondering why this moth was connecting to her so intently, she noticed that she was laying eggs on her hand! This was why we came to her in this way and why we stayed with her three days. We knew that leaving these eggs with her would open her mind and heart to receive all potential gifts contained within it. This was my "birthday gift" to her.

After laying the eggs, the moth stayed on her hand most of the following day, crawling back on whenever Madre tried to set her off. That night before going to bed, Madre put her on a straw hat next to where she had placed the eggs for their incubation period. When Madre got up the next day, the moth was gone, never to be found. (We left through the same portal we had used to arrive.)

The eggs' usual incubation period is eight to eleven days, but my birthday was coming up in thirteen days—December 7, 2021—so these eggs were going to hatch on that day, and I made that clearly known. To celebrate my birthday, I asked Madre to let me tell her what I wanted to do that day, like always. She was told *not* to keep looking at the moth eggs because they would be hatched when we returned home from my birthday outing.

We went to Turtle Beach for sunset and sat with the waves, listening to music. The bike ride down there was rugged, and we had to go through deep water and mud. But after listening to the music of Jason Aldean and chilling on the beach, the return ride was fun and filled with joy! My Madre blasted through the water puddles like the child we have always embodied.

We came back into town and had some gelato before going home. And, as promised, the eggs had hatched! My Madre could hardly believe her eyes, but the miracle of dozens of baby moth larvae was covering the hat and hibiscus leaves. The tiny worms only lived three days and then were completely devoured by cleaner ants who found them before Madre could get a container made to keep them safe. She was so upset over this loss!

But she opened her mind and heart to know the message hidden within this tragic happening, and soon after she heard this:

Spencpiration #3
Accept all things—even those you don't desire or agree with. Judge no thing.

Nature is complex, however, and is always operating in cooperation rather than competition. Ants just did what ants do. My Madre knew the moth was a messenger and that there was a reason she had chosen to lay her eggs on her hand. She also knew the momma moth was me in another form.

Madre later realized the connection with Shima and the moth. Shima is divine feminine, and in being that, is also divine mother. The most sacred of all relationships is the one between a mother and her child, and Shima will continue to support my Madre as she grieves for me. The hardest thing she ever did in her lifetime was watch me suffer, so letting me go was the only choice to end my suffering. The cycle of that lifetime for me was complete, and I do not suffer where I am now. When I was in the hospital in 2012 because of the RSV, my Madre was never far from me, and we were always connected energetically and telepathically while

I was fighting to live every day. While we were there, she wrote this poem to express her *feelings*.

"Sacred Tears"
Gina Gayle Gray

The tears that I shed when my child is in pain
Cleanse my Soul like a much-needed rain.
They start to well up like a pool in my eyes
As the storm cloud of pain comes after my child.

I find myself having to put up a dam
So I can hold back the wall while I conjure a plan.
I have to stay strong while I'm crumbling inside;
My child needs me now 'til his pain subsides.

When I've done all I can to lighten his load,
I can slip away and head down that road,
Where I'm free to release the flood held inside
For the sake of my child, who lives by my side.

I enter the garden and walk the labyrinth
Searching for answers while convulsing within.
I let the tears roll down my face without shame.
They are as pure as the child for whom they came.

We shared a close connection with moths and butterflies when I was living in my body. We raised several butterflies when we lived in the country in Texas. The caterpillars showed up on the parsley in our garden, and we collected them and put them in jars to watch the alchemical process. It was always such a sight to see the beautiful blue and black butterflies emerge! Once they did, we spent a few moments with them as their wings dried, and they crawled on us until they were strong enough to spread their wings and fly away. These were cherished moments while sharing in this cycle of life—*connected freedom*!

I shared another special connection with a butterfly who was taking its final breaths when we stayed in the jungle in Belize. This was an "owl butterfly" and she was brought to me to spend her last moments in my company. My Mama and I agreed that no living thing deserves to be alone as it leaves physical existence. I held her until she folded her wings and dropped her body. It was a beautiful moment of connection, and she assured me that she would be nearby to return the favor of compassionate companionship during my time of need—and she did. This was yet another moment of *connected freedom*.

Moths and butterflies are special messengers. When one shows up, it is reminding you that now is the time to tune in and use your intuition—your inner knowing—to guide you. Remember to raise your vibration often by opening your 360 emotional receptor sites, which are like portals at every degree around you. This allows light and sound frequencies carrying emotions to enter your awareness. When you do this, you're tuned to the frequency of your Soul and your Spirits, Guides, and Guards—including moths and butterflies! The appearance of a moth, butterfly, or an ant is meant to bring you a message of encouragement—a reminder that life is cyclical, every day has meaning, and each moment has potential. Even our last moment. You are always in community with others. Every ending creates a new beginning. Awaken to these messages, because the emotions you will feel are the messengers used by Spirit. Emotions are the language of Spirit. Feel the vibration and seek the highest you can every moment.

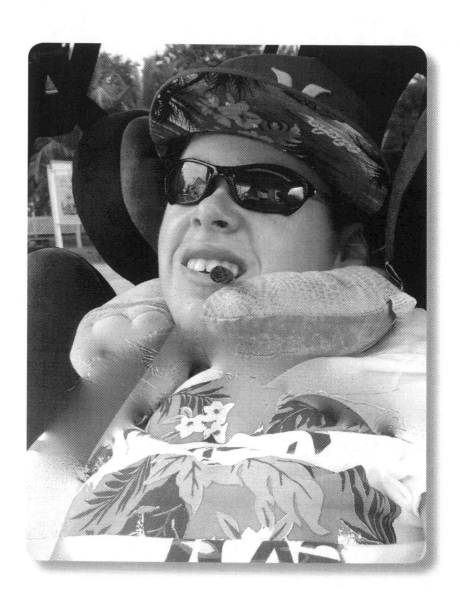

4

MIRACLES AND MAGIC

WHEN DID YOU STOP "KNOWING" THAT MIRACLES HAPPEN EVERY day? I want to share some stories with you about how *believing is seeing* when it comes to miracles and magic.

Most people are programmed to believe that miraculous things only happen when certain people or special Spirit entities make them. I can assure you this is not the case. And many people who spend time in a body that doesn't function properly will understand easily what I'm about to share.

The imagination is a powerful gift, and using it to create entertainment, enjoyment, comfort, happiness, and connection is something I mastered while I was still in my body. Any human can remember how to create miraculous, magical, joyful scenes in his or her life. I used this gift often during my final days because I was neither here nor there, and while in that great in between, I was able to create several miracles.

My favorite Earth Angel I encountered while being Spencer was Jessica. She took care of me for several years, and there are millions of things she did for me, which were all done with kindness, gentleness, and care. Jessica is beautiful inside and out!

She has crystal-clear blue eyes (my favorite color) and the brightest golden energy bubble that she floats around in.

Every day, when she came in to wake me up, she lit up my room with her joyful presence. She was always patient with me as I communicated my wants and needs to her and was one of the best ever at **Listening to the Silence**. She created playlists of my favorite music, painted my trucks according to my specifications, read books with me, made yummy desserts with me (we both loved sweets), took me outside to drive my truck, and showered me with her complete attention every day.

After I went to the hospital the day before I left my physical existence, I wanted to experience Jessica's tender touch. I longed to see her beautiful face again before I transcended. But I had already said my "see you when I see you" to her a few days earlier at my house. So, I had to create a "miracle Jessica" to bring myself a few more moments of communion with her.

My final night in this lifetime was spent in a hospital room with my Dad. Mama had gone home for a few hours to make meals for me. My Dad was exhausted, and I was having great difficulties. We knew we were near the end and needed to get through this long night. The nurses who are in attendance at a time like this are *white light angels*. I knew how to call them in from all my hospital experiences during my lifetime. This was a night when I needed to make some magic happen, so I called in Jessica, aka Jesse. (To help you know the power of my story, the Hebrew name Jesse literally means blessing or miracle!)

When the new shift of nurses came on duty, I manifested "miracle nurse Jessica." She was sweet, with blonde hair and blue eyes, gentle, and beautiful and was the last nurse to care for me as Spencer. When my Mama came back to the hospital, the first person she met was nurse Jessica, and the moment she began giving her report on my condition, Mama was comforted by her genuine compassion and care. Then she read her name tag, which of course said Jessica, and she realized what I had created and knew why I did.

I really enjoy creating magical miracles, and the reason is because they remind people to *feel* hope and joy. The experience of a miracle is open to everyone! You only need to "remember you know" to see one.

The collaborative nature of miracles is one of my favorite aspects of them. The energies that must be joined together to pull off a miracle are many. This usually means several agreements are made between individuals who will play a role in creating the event. I like to use dreamtime to connect with Souls, Spirits, Guides, and Guards who will all be invited to participate in the miracle I'm creating.

One of the greatest miracles I created after dropping my body was finding the perfect family to buy the home where I had spent most of my physical life at 329 Country Court. As I mentioned earlier, I took an active role in selling our home and assured my Mama that once she put the house on the market, I would find the buyers, send them there, and that she would know for certain who they were when they appeared. This miracle manifested rapidly exactly how I intended, and it had several undeniable magical signs that it was taking place. As I had said, the buyers would be known when they appeared, and the third family to look at the home bought it! The wife and mother of the family is named Gina—the same name as my Mama! Gina's mother's name is Gayle—my Mama's middle name.

This Gina grew up riding horses—like my Mama—and wanted to share the experience with her children, which was one of the reasons she wanted a home like ours. Gina and her husband have three young children and were all along for the initial viewing of our home. They were so excited and happy while they explored the house, especially once they were upstairs, where all the bedrooms are. They each chose their bedroom and announced to their parents that they had made the decision; this was going to be their new home! And it was so.

The only difficulty in creating this miracle was keeping my Mama in a state of hopefulness and knowing that this family would be buying our home. The family had just begun their search, so ours was the first house they looked at. Even though the children knew this was their new home, the adults decided to practice due diligence and look at other options. During this time period, I reassured my Mama that this sale would happen, and she only needed patience and a strong belief in this miracle. I let her know weekly that I was visiting the oldest child during dreamtime to help him help me create this miracle for all of us. It was easy to play with him in his dreams because we share a love for jaguars, and my nocturnal jaguar friends enjoy dreamtime adventures. The family quickly made a cash offer, and the deal was set to close on November 23, 2020—no coincidence with the date! I've dedicated an entire chapter in this book to how I use numbers to send messages and the number twenty-three is my favorite.

When my Mama took the keys and final papers over to the new Gina at 329 Country Court, their children were wearing their costumes from Halloween. The younger boy was wearing a bear costume. The older boy was wearing a "big cat" one, and my Mama asked him what kind of big cat he was. He answered with a big, "Grrrrrrrrr! I'm a *jaguar!*" and all Mama could say back was, "of course you are!"

She quickly put all the pieces into place and saw the big picture of this miracle I—in collaboration with many others—had created for the greatest good of *all*. Our amazing home has a new family to love it. Mama and Dad were able to move toward having less to deal with, and the new Gina's family has an amazing place to call home. As a bonus, they even agreed to adopt our cats, Gary and Baggy, so they didn't have to move.

Miracles and magic come in all forms and range in size from tiny to grand. I mastered creating miracles when I was still in my body and traveling across Texas in our RV named Thor with my Dad and our friend Joe. Whenever we went on a road trip, I always partnered with Archangel Michael to ensure we were protected every mile along the way. I could manifest a roadside mechanic who could work on any aspect of a motor home like our Thor anywhere we happened to experience a need. We had tire problems often, usually on the trailer being pulled behind Thor, but sometimes on Thor too. The number of times we received a roadside miracle on our trips is too many to count, but they all mattered and counted as miracles!

One of the grandest miracles I pulled off during my earth years was surviving RSV in 2012 and leaving the hospital in record time after having tracheostomy surgery. When I decided to sign the addendum to my Soul Contract and stay another seven years, that was a complex agreement. And this agreement involved other Souls as well—my Mama and my Dad. My choice to take that path involved a great unfolding of my being as I endured total dependence on others for my comfort and literally for my life during my final seven years. Since I now had no voice, I had no way to contact anyone if I had a need. Before my tracheostomy, I could make sound, but after, I had no voice. I was completely silent for the next seven years, so someone had to have eyes on me at all times.

The backup for me was the telepathic abilities Mama and I shared then and still share now. I always *felt* the knowing that Mama would be there for me until the end with this new agreement coming into effect. Our agreement was made in **the place called love** and was created in complete **grateful connection**, which is a powerful energy that is still alive for us today. She knew how to **Listen to the Silence,** and once my voice was taken from me, the tuning of our heart strings became very important. Whenever I needed her, I'd send my SOS to her heart, which was always open to me. Mama had to be tuned in to be able to hear me in the silence of her Spirit Soul because that's where my messages came to her.

All my people—Mama, Dad, and Jessica—had to pass tests to prove they could take care of me before the hospital would release me to go home when I had RSV in 2012. We had spent sixty days in ICU, and then they expected us to stay an additional sixty days in the trach care unit to learn how to care for my new condition. My people passed their tests and made a break for it after ten days.

We were denied an ambulance transport from the hospital to our home because the hospital employee empowered with directing our discharge didn't agree with the doctor who decided to let us go home. Her attempt to punish us or create a barrier to our plan failed. We checked out according to our own timeline and created an escape plan for getting home according to our terms.

Our "getaway ride" was our neighbor Tom's motor home that was fully charged, set up, and ready to escort me home as soon as we left the hospital parking garage. We met in the parking lot across the street, and I was put in the motor home for a comfortable ride to my home where I recovered very quickly. I never used oxygen once I left the hospital environment, and one by one, the prescriptions for medicines and the need for outside people and equipment was eliminated.

Within a few weeks we had discontinued the help that had been prescribed because they did not help my condition at all. My Mama began learning about all the new labels that were put on me, such as "failure to thrive," "respiratory patient," "ventilator dependent," and many other limiting condition labels that were designed to prevent us from living life. This was the beginning of a chapter in life—my final one—and we chose to see it as an **all-you-can-*live* buffet**, filled with opportunities and potential in front of us. At one end of the table sat courage and at the opposite end sat fear. We chose to focus on the end that offered courage serving up the potential to go beyond merely surviving to a place of shining brightly.

The grand miracle that was created then was that I was able to live another seven years. The prognosis the staff at the hospital gave was that I would only live a few days once I went home. However, the reality we created took us on an airplane ride to another country within six weeks of coming home from the hospital! Before I had become ill, we had travelled to Belize and bought a villa on the beach, and my family had plans to spend time there. I wasn't going to be the reason we couldn't go. My desire to get back there was one of my greatest motivators, and we focused on this every day while I was in ICU. My Mama pinned photos from our first trip there all over the curtain in my room, and we talked about our plans to return there with everyone who came in to care for me.

Getting back there took an act of courage and was a collaborative grand miracle! I needed someone to carry all my equipment and supplies while my Dad carried me for us to move about. So, we expanded our village and all got on a plane to travel to the beach for a few days in June 2012. This trip was my reason for recovering. I had somewhere I planned to be and people who were counting on me to make it there.

This was not an easy miracle to manifest. There was a lot to learn, and we dove head-first into the deep end of the ocean, trusting our Spirits, Guides, and Guards. Fear was not an option, and when my Mama and I put our efforts and desires together, we cocreate anything we choose. I chose to continue to *live* my life because as Jason Aldean sings, "Every man dies, but not every man lives." I intended to live fully … and I did everything they said I would never do, with the help of my village!

It is our deepest hope that others reading about my messages and miracles will open to all the miracles and magic that happen in your lives every day. Sharing brightness and joy are easy for the stars in the cosmos, and when we all remember that each of us is powered by our own star in the cosmos as well, we will naturally raise the voltage of each other symbiotically. Our connection to each other is real. We are all connected energetically, as are the stars in the cosmos. Remember how to *feel* this **connected freedom** to each other and to all of creation. Celebrate your own great potential every day, but also remember that when you are **gratefully connected** to others, that potential is expanded, and grand miracles can then be created.

Another miracle that I created in collaboration with other Souls, Spirits, Guides, and Guards was getting back to see my jaguar friends Junior Buddy and Lucky Boy, who lived at the zoo in Belize. This was a grand miracle that was met with complete resistance by everyone who was available at the time it was originally being discussed. No one wanted to go back to Belize on an airplane because our last trip in 2014 had ended in stressful chaos at the airport, and there was no one left in "that village" to help with another trip. We attempted to create this grand miracle for three years with no success. My Mama even worked on getting her pilot's license and looked into buying a plane to fly us there. But that didn't happen for many reasons, so the plan that did succeed was this. We purchased a motor home to drive back to Belize. We spent many hours cocreating this grand miracle and sending gratitude to the cosmos for working with us to find someone who could drive us in a motor home across Mexico to Belize from Texas! The help wanted ad we put out to the cosmos read like this: Looking for someone to escort a young man and his Mama from Texas to Belize in a motor home. This person needs to speak Spanish fluently, be fearless and a bit crazy, and must be able to provide protection and security for safe passage across Mexico. The ability to protect and serve precious lives seeking adventure is nonnegotiable.

We found a Belizean man who was known locally as Rambo, and he became my Sherpa of sorts.

When creating a miracle, the most important aspect of it is to give birth to it! To do this, becoming fully immersed in the energy of the experience is necessary. Nurturing it when it's an idea with unwavering focus and intention is a process that I mastered when I was in my earth body. To see a grand miracle come to life, you must spend a great deal of time living in the energy of its actuation. This use of imagination to facilitate manifestation is something I was well known for.

This grand miracle was created and experienced fully, and what an adventure it was! The motor home we found was perfect, and I named it the Spencermobile. We packed enough supplies for the drive across Mexico and to live in Belize for six months and set out on our incredible adventure on February 23, 2018. The date has meaning of course since it is again the number twenty-three. Our journey to Belize took ten days, and we lived six months in our villa on the beach. The experience was an amazing journey. As we drove across Mexico, we were stopped often by local, state, or federal officers. I rode perched in my copilot seat up front while Mama did the driving. We gave the appearance of vulnerability to some of these Mexicans at stop points who are known to solicit money for safe passage from foreign travelers. However, whenever they stopped us with malicious intent, upon entering our Spencermobile, when they slid our side door open, they were met by our secret weapon, Rambo! I did my part as well and always wore my ranger beret, which was given to me by my badass cousin, Drew, whenever we were stopped at these check points along the way! I also kept my machete on my lap, so I wielded my own energetic power of protection coming directly from our travel partner, Archangel Michael. The result was, we traveled safely across Mexico in a black Mercedes Winnebago without ever feeling we were in danger or even threatened.

This trip was on my bucket list, and the most important aspect of making it was so I could have my Mama all to myself. I wanted this time with her alone without all the distractions of her busy life in Texas. I had tried for years to get her to fire all the help so that she and I could take care of each other. It was my desire to see her relax and enjoy herself without having to work so hard every day. Most importantly, I wanted to see her laugh again because she had lost her connection to her joy, and I knew I could help her reconnect if I had her to myself for a while.

We absolutely rediscovered our joy together! Even though Mama doesn't fully realize the powerful impact that trip had on me, I want her to know it was absolutely perfect from my point of view. We spent every day and night together for six months, living life according to our own terms. We lived on the beach enjoying the sea breeze and watching the moonrise over the ocean. We visited my jaguar friends at the zoo, and zookeeper Sharon Matola took us on a private tour of the hidden parts where many other jaguars live that no one else ever gets to see. I was able to visit the zoo again for a night tour, and that was an amazing adventure I will always cherish. We stayed in the jungle a few nights and I was able to enjoy many hours breathing on my own without the help of the ventilator because the air quality was so fresh and clean. I got to take a bath in an outdoor tub one night under the light of a full moon. I don't know many people who can say they've done that!

I got my ear pierced so I could wear a diamond stud like Jason Aldean, and I got a tattoo to honor the girl who was special to me. I drank Tito's on the beach and listened to my music all day sitting under the palapa. I celebrated the birth of an amazing Belizean man affectionately known as Papa Puche and drank rum with him at his eightieth birthday party. I felt like a man instead of a helpless person when I was in the care of my Sherpa, who treated me like his equal when we lived in Belize. We are forever *gratefully connected*. After this book is published, I plan to write another one sharing all the experiences we had during my great Belizean adventure that I lived during the first six months of my final year of my life as Spencer.

Spencpiration #4

*Allow others to live their own truth without
judging them, trying to fix them,
helping them, or hurting them.*

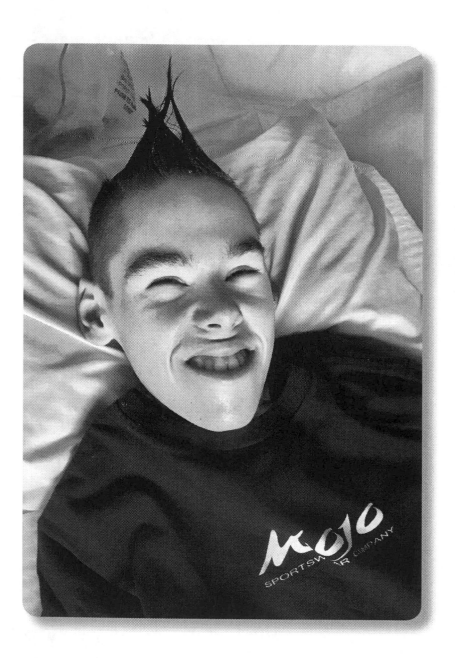

5

SPEAKING THROUGH SONGS

My favorite way to talk to my people when I was in my earth suit was using song lyrics. I couldn't speak words, use my hands to make sign language, or make use of any speaking device. My mind worked much faster than my ability to manually activate any device, so I chose to use other ways to communicate. I used the lyrics of songs to get my thoughts delivered as messages that my people could hear and understand.

I started doing this when I was very young. The first time I used this method was one day when my Madre and I were listening to Montgomery Gentry, and they sang their song "Gone." We had a family friend who had lived with us for many months, worked for my Dad, and was my Madre's closest friend for many years. Her name was Amy. She had joined the Coast Guard and moved away, and we hadn't seen her for many months. I missed her greatly.

Troy Gentry sang

> *"She's gone! Gone like a freight train, gone like yesterday, gone like a soldier in the civil war. Gone like a 59 Cadillac, like all the good things that ain't never*

47

*comin' back. She's gone, gone, gone! Packed her bags
and now she's gone."*

I got Madre's attention and let her know that song made
me think of Amy and how much I was missing her, and she
understood exactly what I was saying! We lay on the floor, cried
together, and talked about Amy for a long time.

Soon after, my beautiful friend Jessica came into my life. She
and I listened to music every day when she came to help care for
me. We spent many hours during the day finding songs we both
enjoyed, and when there was a lyric being sung that said exactly
what I wanted to say to someone, I let her know I wanted that
song to be put on my playlist. My Madre still has this playlist on
her iPod!

As I was creating this way of communicating with people, I
let Jessica know that I wanted to go into my Madre's office so I
could tell her something important. Jessica played the song I was
asking her to repeat, and Madre listened to it until she knew what
I wanted to say. As she listened to the song (or songs) over and
over, she would watch my face so she could read my reaction to
the words being spoken within the lyrics. There were times when
we would have multiple songs that needed to be deciphered in this
way so my message could be understood completely. We worked
together as a team, and once I was heard, Madre could go back
to work, and Jessica and I would go on with our day.

This way of using music worked very well for me because
throughout the years, all my people learned how to listen to the
lyrics of songs I wanted to hear and to watch my face for my
clear "yes" when something was said that I wanted to say. My
favorite artists were country singers because they are easy to
understand, and they're great storytellers. However, I could find a
message in many songs since I was a great listener. This method of
communicating my wants, needs, and desires became even more
important once I had my tracheostomy and was no longer able to

make any sound. I practiced my intentional listening to song lyrics every day and was grateful that we always had a great variety of singers and songs playing. This gave me an expanded vocabulary to choose from, and I used it to my advantage so I could say many things that I couldn't have otherwise. My physical situation was complex. I was a nonverbal communicator while I was in my physical body, and my only communication limitation was an inability to express myself verbally. My receptive communication skills were intact and enhanced greatly since I spent my entire life listening. This is also the case with many other nonverbal communicators who are living in this way in many forms. It's unfortunate when speaking people assume that nonverbal communicators can't understand what is being said around and about them while disregarding their ability to perceive the meaning of the words they're speaking. I hope this book opens awareness to the potential of all nonverbal people to speak without words. When they do, heart-centered communication with and without words will be improved.

Song lyrics became my greatest resource for communicating with my people once I had a tracheostomy. My cuff was always inflated on my tube, so I was not able to make any sound. It's complicated and hard to explain, but this was my choice and part of my addendum to my Soul Contract when I agreed to stay another seven years.

My relationship with my tracheostomy tube and ventilator was emotionally heavy. I had enjoyed complete freedom from illness or injury the first sixteen years of my life, and I had no need for any medical equipment of any kind before my experience with RSV.

My dependency on all this stuff was difficult to accept. When I first saw photos of myself with the tracheostomy tube connected to the ventilator coming out of my neck, I refused to look at them. Even when I was having a good day and didn't need the ventilator, seeing the tube when looking in the mirror or in photos bothered me. My Mama **Listened to the Silence** and heard me about this. She would slip my shirt over my trach when she took pictures or would use Photoshop to remove it from photos of me whenever she could.

I found a song that expressed how I *felt* about my tracheostomy and ventilator while listening to music my Mama had downloaded from an episode of *The Voice* after we watched the show one day. I let her know that song was saying how I *felt* by first getting her attention while it was playing. I would do this by clacking my teeth together. Once she acknowledged me, I smiled and nodded so the song would get played over and over until the message was heard clearly. This song was called "Mercy" and was sung by a cute young lady named Juhi.

She sang

> *I love you, but I'm on my knees, beggin' please stop playin' games! I don't know what this is, but you got me good! I'm under your spell. I'm beggin' you for mercy! Why won't you release me? Ya got me beggin' you for mercy! Why won't you release me? Mercy!*

As she's belting out these words, I raised my chin up so Mama knew I was singing this song to my damn trach, begging it for mercy and asking for it to release me! Another day, Mama and I were watching the band Train perform a concert on TV. When they sang the song "Calling All Angels," I let her know there was a message to hear in those song lyrics.

They sang

> *I'm calling all you Angels! I won't give up if you don't give up! I won't give up if you don't give up! I need a sign to know you are here. **I want a reason for the way things have to be!** I need a hand to know there's some kind of hope inside of me!*

We listened to this song at least ten times and cried while Mama held my hands up in the air, calling to the angels. I wanted to be free of my trach and ventilator and was begging the angels to help me. I wanted to have my prior life back where I wasn't a burden to everyone who was tasked with taking care of me. I wanted my voice back so I could at least make the sound of laughter. I wanted my joy back so I could *feel* the sound of laughter. These moments with beautiful song lyrics gave me the opportunity to express how I *felt* about my silence and my situation, and that was empowering.

Another perfect song came along for me to share how my life was being experienced inside my world of complete helplessness and silence. I needed a machine to assist me with every breath I took; a tube in my throat to keep me from drowning in my own saliva; a tube in my stomach to give me food for nourishment and water for hydration; and a machine to suction crap out of my throat and lungs. I was completely dependent on others to meet all my needs in order to stay alive.

There were times I became depressed because the struggles of every moment were real. I never had a breath that came easy for me even before the RSV that led to the trach and vent, but I was now living a life of suffering beyond the struggles I had known my first sixteen years. I desperately wanted my prior life of freedom from the trach tube and ventilator. I didn't think that was asking too much!

Sia came out with her song "Alive," and the first time I heard it, I once again let Mama know those lyrics were about my life! Sia sings

> *I wanted everything I never had. Like the love that comes with (an easy) life. I wore envy and I hated that, but I survived! I had a one-way ticket to the place where the demons go. No hope, just lies, and you're taught to cry in your pillow, but I survived! I'm still breathin', I'm*

still breathin', I'm still breathin'! I'm alive! I'm alive!
I'm alive! Took me down, but I'm still breathin.' You
took it all, but I'm still breathin.' I took and I took, and
I took what you gave, but you never noticed that I was
in pain. **I knew what I wanted, I went out and got**
it. Did all the things that you said that I wouldn't!
I told you that I would never be forgotten!

This song became my anthem. I lived those lyrics and fought hard for every single breath I took while I was in my earth suit.

When we left the hospital after getting my tracheostomy, and they told us we wouldn't be able to do all the things we had done before, we just smiled and pretended we were planning to comply with all the restrictions they attempted to put on us. From the moment I was carried into my home at 329 Country Court, I never needed supplemental oxygen because our air was purified by the one hundred-plus oak trees on our property. Thank you, tree beard Spirit!

Within a few weeks of leaving the hospital, we had discontinued all the prescriptions that had been sent home with us, and I was outside visiting my horses and learning how to do all the things that they said I would never do—just like Sia sings in her song. I was still breathin' and I stayed *alive* for seven more years!

During those last seven years, several different helpers came into my life. Many didn't last very long because my Madre was definitely a "Mama jaguar" who did not tolerate anyone making a mistake when it came to my care. Some of them could not earn my trust even though they meant well, and I always let it be known that I wasn't comfortable being left alone in their care. We tried a variety of people over the years with different personalities and qualities, and I always enjoyed their company. However, occasionally, when someone was very uncomfortable—either because watching me suffer was painful or too much pressure for them, or they were intimidated by Mama—problems would arise.

I had one such helper who didn't know when to stop talking, and there were many days when I needed to sleep a lot, so this created a problem. This was a guy, and I really appreciated it when we had a guy around because he could talk to me about things that I was interested in. But this guy was *never* quiet, so I called my Mama in one day and let her know he was driving me crazy. She knew it because her office was next to my bedroom, and he drove her crazy too. He just did not know how to sit in silence, even for a moment. Mama and I had a talk about this when we went to bed that night, and while we were talking, I kept lifting my chin, showing her my trach. She finally figured out that I was telling her I wished my helper, the guy who never stopped talking, had a trach because if he did, he wouldn't have a voice! We had a good laugh about this, and of course it was our inside joke that we never said to him because it would have hurt his feelings.

I had another chatty helper who was dear to me and was in my life for a few years. She also was never able to stop talking, and one day when Mama and I were listening to music in bed as we often did, we were playing a new Christina Aguilera album. We heard

> *So, for once, why don't you just shut up! Shut the f@*k up! Shut up! Shut the f@*k up! You keep runnin' your mouth. You like the sound of your voice. So why don't you just shut up!*

Leave it to Christina Aguilera to sing me a perfect song to express what I wanted to say to my talkative helpers! I called on this song many times to let it be known that people were talking too much and saying too little. This is also one of the songs I sent to my Madre telepathically during my final twenty-three days when I was in my darkest days of suffering before I dropped my body. I needed to let her know that hearing people talk had become disturbing to me and was disrupting my transcendence process. Once I sent her this message, she **Listened to the Silence** as always and heard me clearly.

From that day forward I told her who I wanted to come to see me so I could have my final moments with them one at a time. I couldn't tolerate any more groups of people in my room talking about things that I knew no longer mattered to me and shouldn't matter to them. I used telepathy only during my final days because I was suffering deeply and was in much pain. I couldn't engage with anyone to respond in my usual way to questions, so my only communication was wordless thought forms I sent to my Mama and Dad. Once I let it be known that I had seen who I wanted to see one last time, no one else was invited into our home to see me. My aunt Vicki and Ms. Joan were the only people besides Mama and Dad that I saw those last few days. They were our *white light angels* who opened their hearts to each of us while we all suffered together.

During my last week I wasn't in my body much, but I was sharing my transition experience with my Mama. I used song titles and lyrics, shared visions showing her where my Spirit Soul was "out there, neither here nor there," and spoke poetry to her. She was completely dialed in to my communications because I had spent many years preparing her for this time—and beyond. She **Listened to the Silence** and documented our conversations and my transition experience. One night while I was in the bathtub, which was one of the only places I found a tiny bit of relief from my intense pain and the heaviness of my body, I sent my Mama a message using Jason Aldean's song, "My Kinda Party."

I played these lyrics in her mind:

> *Words got it there's gonna be a party! You can find me on the back of a jacked-up tailgate watching all these pretty things. I'll find peace at the bottom of a real tall cold drink, listening to some Skynard and some old Hank. Let's get this thing started! It's my kinda party!*

She saw clearly that I wasn't in my pain body at that time, and when she heard the lyrics in her mind, she asked me if I was at a party "out there." I answered *yes*! When the guitar solo started, I told her to play this song for everyone and have them see me as *this* guy playing *my* guitar on the tailgate of a pickup truck at *my kinda party* after I'm gone. She knew I was already there because my Spirit Soul was barely hanging on by this time.

The next day I asked for my Jason Aldean playlist to be put on shuffle and that no one talk in my presence anymore. I needed to focus on transcending, and I wanted to be serenaded by Jason because his music had been so important to me most of my lifetime. His voice soothed me and carried me into the wave of joy where the density of my body wasn't experienced. His songs are full of clear messages that he conveys with passion and power to his listeners. And he plays a guitar as if it's part of his body, using it to give the notes that he's singing a ride on the guitar strings! I told my Mama that when they heard the song "Blacktop Gone," I would be leaving. We had 113 songs on that playlist, and it played for many hours well into the night. My aunt Vicki and Mama took turns writing down every song title as they played, and we all, including my Dad, listened closely to the lyrics. I was at the front row at his best and longest concert ever given! I was dancing, cheering, waving my arms, playing my guitar, and singing along with every song.

The *last song* to play was "Blacktop Gone," and as it played, Mama, Dad, and Vicki hovered over me, crying and telling me I was free to go. But when the song finished, the iPod died—but I stayed another three days.

In that moment of confusion, I said to my Mama, *Now I have your complete attention, and if you stay focused, I will bring you with me and show you things that you need to know.*

Then I showed her a split-second image of what my face *would look like* after I dropped my body. She was devastated but stayed strong in that moment, and the day that I did leave, she recognized the vision immediately. She stayed focused and because of that, our journey together has continued in the **realm called love that is a place I now call home**. I will share more about this later (and so will she).

The song "Blacktop Gone" came out when Madre and I lived on the beach in Belize in 2018. When we first arrived there, our Spencermobile engine had to be repaired, so we were unable to explore and were trapped at our tiny beach villa for several weeks. That was not our plan; we had taken this journey to have an adventure and sitting on the beach every day became boring. I wanted to see the jungles, go to the zoo to see the jaguars, and get out onto the ocean to see some dolphins. While we were lamenting on the beach one day, we were listening to Jason Aldean's new album, *Rearview Town*.

The song "Blacktop Gone" was speaking my words:

> *One horse town. Restless Soul! You know the first chance I get I'm blacktop gone! Four-lane fast. Toppin' off the tank with some never look back. Chase that sun, race that wind! Whip them horses that you can't fence in. Free like a freeway! High on a highway. Crankin' up a getaway song. Gettin' blacktop gone!*

I let Madre know that this song was how I felt about being stuck without our ride and that as soon as we got it back, we would be blacktop gone! We had a great laugh about it and agreed. We played this song several times a day every day until we got our Spencermobile back. Then, the minute we did, we put this song on the stereo, cranked it up, and hit the road heading for the jungle where I discovered I could breathe for many hours without my ventilator.

My love for Jason Aldean was deep … much deeper than anyone could fully understand. But my Madre gave attention to the clues I gave about my relationship with the highest aspect of him along the way. One day while we were listening to his music on the beach, we had a talk about how many lifetimes she and I had experienced together, and how many more we would have to come. She asked me if I wanted to "come back" as Jason Aldean, and I told her that I *was* Jason already! She realized I was talking about other realms that some refer to as parallel realities where we coexist. Once she understood this, she asked me if she could sing and perform with me on stage in that realm. I told her no, because she can't sing well in this reality or the others! So, then she asked if she could at least sing backup. Again, I told her no, even that wasn't possible. Then she asked if her role was still to be my "roadie" who's responsible for managing my affairs and carrying my gear. I answered yes, so we had a good laugh about this!

I continued using Jason Aldean song titles and lyrics after I transcended because I knew I would be heard.

When my Mama returned to our home after I dropped my body, I immediately sent her the message to start our Jason playlist on shuffle. The first song I sang to her was called "I'll See You When I See You," and I meant it!

The lyrics were the perfect message:

> *Let's don't say goodbye. I hate the way it sounds. So if you don't mind, let's just say for now, see you when I see you. Another place, some other time. If I ever get down your way, or you're ever up around mine, we'll laugh about the old days and catch up on the new. Yeah, I'll see you when I see you ... and I hope it's someday real soon.*

After listening to this song, my Mama sat outside my bedroom in complete silence while I completed my transcendence, which included my final departure from her body. As part of my process, I had to "cut the cord" that connected me to my physical existence.

This connection was in her womb, which is where I began my journey within her body twenty-three years earlier.

A Spirit Soul must do this, or it will remain tethered to the earth realm. My connection to earth was firmly grounded through my Mama. She was and always will be my Madre de la Tierra. She *felt* the intense pain in the depth of her Spirit Soul in the center of her body as the final remnants of my physicality went dark and my Spirit Soul released into the True Light with Shima. Once this was complete, I guided her awareness to her heart above her solar plexus and whispered to her that although our time together had come to an end as earth son and Mama, I was always with her in her heart and our Spirit Souls would reunite very soon. Then I told her I wanted her to go to my social media and write this message to my friends to let them know I had left: "I'm Blacktop Gone ... to My Kinda Party ... and I'll See You When I See You"! I wanted everyone to know I was now living my life as Jason Aldean, singing all his songs and playing guitar as good or better than him now!

Most everyone I knew during my earth days was aware of my love for Jason's music. I discovered in my freedom to soar all realms in the cosmos that I now have complete access to the "cosmic jukebox in the sky," as I call it, so I can send songs to my people anytime I choose—and I do.

One of my favorites to use to remind people to get out and live their earth life with as much enjoyment as possible is Jason's song "Not Every Man Lives."

It says

> *Have you ever loved someone that you would die for?*
> *Have you ever chased a dream too high to reach and*
> *pulled it in? The truth is, every man dies, but not every*
> *man lives! I want to paint outside the lines! Run the red*
> *lights in my mind!* **Take everything one lifetime has**
> **to give.** *I want to stand inside the fire! Walk blindfolded*

on the wire! Every man dies, but not every man lives.
Have you ever thought about how fast time passes? Ever
thought about what you would leave behind? Ever stood
up for something you believed in and drawn the line?

I had many obstacles in my lifetime that could have easily given me legitimate excuses to stop living. But that was not the path I chose! My parents made sure I kept going even though the days were long, and the nights were even longer. We worked as a team, along with many other people who came into my life during my twenty-three years in an earth suit that really didn't work very well. My dependency on others was experienced as **grateful connection** where there was always an exchange of the essence of love that was the currency I used to pay my way in life. Music and song lyrics helped me express my love and gratitude to the people who cared for me, and this way of communicating didn't end when my time on earth did. I can—and still do—send people songs to deliver messages often, and most of the time, those who know me best hear me. My Madre and sister, Alexis, went to Mexico a few months after I dropped my body in 2019 to have some much-needed time together.

One day, as my Madre was walking to the beach, I captured her attention with a song that was playing over the speakers in the hotel lobby.

She heard the lyrics being sung by Celine Dion

> *For all those times you stood by me, for all the truth that*
> *you made me see. For all the joy you brought to my life,*
> *for all the wrong that you made right. For every dream*
> *you made come true, for all the love I found in you,*
> ***I'll be forever thankful! You're the one who held***
> ***me up, never let me fall.*** *You're the one who saw me*
> *through, through it all. You were my strength when I*
> *was weak, **you were my voice when I couldn't speak**,*

you saw the best there was in me. Lifted me up when I couldn't reach. You gave me faith cause you believed. I'm everything I am because you loved me! You gave me wings and made me fly, you touched my hand I could touch the sky. I lost my faith you gave it back to me. **You said no star was out of reach!** *You stood by me, and I stood tall! I had your love! I had it all. I'm grateful for each day you gave me! I don't know that much, but I know this much is true. I was blessed because I was loved by you! You were always there for me. The tender wind that carried me.* **The light in the dark, shining your love into my life.** *You've been my inspiration. My world was a better place because of you!*

She sat on the sofa in the lobby and listened to every word, and she knew it was me using this song at that exact moment to tell her how I *feel* about her and how much she means to me.

I continue to use song lyrics and song titles to send messages to Mama and everyone else who has opened their hearts and emotional receptor sites to hear me. I can pop a song onto a car stereo; a home stereo; any Sirius satellite station; a restaurant music system; all public sound systems; to name a few, anytime I desire. I've been given infinite access to the cosmic jukebox in the sky, and I enjoy using it often!

This is one of the best and easiest ways for many Spirit Souls who are on this side of the veil to speak to their people who miss them. Please trust this and tune in and up to hear these messages. All you need to do is dial the frequency of your mind up a notch, ask your loved ones who are in their Spirit Soul now to use a song to say something to you, and then intentionally listen for it during your day. I continue to use it every day with my Mama. As she's listening to me now, so she can scribe this book for me, I'll play a song repeatedly in her mind until she hears what I'm saying to her. It may take a day or two, but I play it until she gets my message completely. The past few days, I've been playing her the song by Train called "Words," and I wanted to remind her that when I left, I was still by her side, *always* and *in all ways*.

We listened to this song often.

> *I'd give anything, but I won't give up on you! I'd say anything, but not goodbye. I'll run with your changes, and **I'm always on your side!** And there's not a word I've heard that would make me change my mind. Words ... they'll try to shake you. Don't let them break you or stop your world from turning. **When words keep you from feeling good, use them as firewood, and let them burn!***

My Mama endured many lonely hours in deep darkness suffering grief and despair after I dropped my body. She soon learned that even though she had no people by her side, she was never alone. I am by her side!

I became empowered in many ways when I dropped my body. The greatest superpower I awakened once I completed my transition process back into my *highly evolved beingness* was my ability to pick my Madre up and carry her when she needed me to. I proudly lifted her up one day when she was experiencing a moment of desperation. She was on the floor in a puddle of hopelessness, crying out to me to help her leave her earth existence because she didn't want to be there anymore.

In that moment I told her to *listen*, and this is what she heard:

> *Oh, give me strength, and give me peace. Does anyone out there want to hear me? It's just another downpour; don't let it get the best of you! **It's only up from the floor, light everything inside of you.** Don't burn out, don't burn out on me!*

These song lyrics were being sung by Imagine Dragons on her stereo, and she needed to *hear those words—which were* my *words*—at that exact time in her moment of great sadness. She *did* listen and got up off the floor and printed out the lyrics of this song called "Burn Out" and then listened to it several more times. She knew in her heart that it wasn't time for her to drop her body because she is needed on GAIA to support others who are walking the same path as her. Our *grateful connection* is alive and well, and together we now can share our experiences so others can open their awareness and expand into this eternal and infinite aspect of all Spirit Souls—both in body and without one.

I also use song titles to send messages to her. One day she was listening to David Lanz piano music and a song touched her deeply. She looked on her iPod to see the title of the song and it was called "Madre de la Tierra," so I let her know then that I honored her greatly for being that to me. She was my Earth Mama and so much more to me infinitely and eternally.

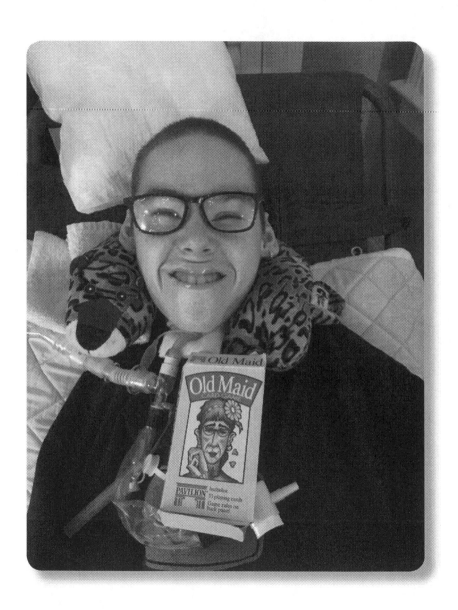

6

PLAYING WITH NUMBERS

THE GIFT OF SPOKEN WORDS THAT WAS ACTIVATED IN HUMANS WAS a special privilege that had great potential. Highly evolved beings (HEBs) do not need spoken words to communicate. They simply share thought forms with each other telepathically using sparks of light frequencies without sound waves to carry the thoughts. Sound is light slowed down. Sadly, this gift has been abused and misused for most of life by those who have chosen to use words maliciously to be in control and to manipulate and harm others. The "tricky tricksters" have used words to cast spells on people's minds and create great confusion while causing harm to each other and destroying relationships.

Spencpiration #5

Anytime you think or say, "I wish that—" followed by anything other than "I," YOU are attempting to control someone else.

As part of my Soul Contract, I agreed to be in an earth suit without the ability to speak words. When I signed the addendum to stay another seven years, it was an agreement to be without the ability to make sound. It was part of my Spirit Soul's evolution, and although it was difficult to see it that way while I was living it, the valuable information I was able to absorb during that time was only available from a state of complete expressive silence. I was aware on a superconscious level that all words, spoken and unspoken, have codes embedded within them. Light codes are paired with sound codes when spoken. Numbers are relevant, as they carry specific frequencies that can be felt as energy—vibration—by humans in physical form using their ordinary sense of hearing. The frequencies of the primary (or root) numbers and letters are simple, while words are more complex. Letters align with specific numbers. My sense of hearing was extremely fine tuned to the emotions that are always gifted along with every word. Every thought begins as a spark of light, and then emotions—the true gifts—are offered to blend with the thought so it can catch a sound wave and be heard and *felt* as a spoken word.

It was during those seven years that I found alternative ways to express my wants, needs, and desires that led to sharpening my telepathic communication skills. I had a lot of time to "observe words" because I was surrounded by people who liked to fill empty space with talking constantly!

Fortunately, my environment was mostly positive, with more harmony than discord. My home was filled with love and beauty inside and out, and this helped me survive my existence. Although I couldn't speak words, I could hear, comprehend, and *feel* every word spoken around me, about me, and to me, and this perspective provided great insight into how people communicate with each other. Please know this: if you are in the presence of a nonverbal communicator in your world, they are *always* listening and learning from your spoken words! And more importantly, they *feel* the emotions of every word you speak—even if you're not.

There are many beings who know how to communicate without words, and I was one such person while I was in my physical form. When I had a voice before I experienced my illness and got a tracheostomy, I could make audible sounds to express myself. I could laugh when I *felt* joy, and I did so often. Laughter is contagious, so everyone could catch that wave! The wave laughter rides *is* joy. I could say "mmmmmm" whenever my Mama was cooking my favorite meals as the smell rose up to where my Dad and I were upstairs. For her, being able to hear and *feel* me express my excitement and gratitude for the delicious food she was going to bring us made all her effort in the kitchen worthwhile. I enjoyed being able to express my love, joy, and gratitude when I could make sounds, and I missed it greatly when I no longer could.

When my voice was silenced, I had to rely on creativity to communicate in other ways. Using numbers became a simpler way for me to express myself. I first discovered a way to say "I love you" to my grandma Evelyn one day when she came to visit me after I had gotten the tracheostomy. She was lying in bed with me, holding my hand and talking with me. She was telling me how much she loved me. My right thumb was the only part of my hand that I could move with intention, so I tapped it on her hand three times while saying "I love you" to her in my mind. She figured it out quickly and was so excited to tell my Mama about this exchange of affection we had cocreated!

I continued using this as often as I could to tell anyone who held my hand how much I loved them. This filled my heart with joy! I especially loved using it every night with my parents. They always held my hand in bed as we went to sleep at night, and this brought me great comfort to be able to tell them how much I love them. I still use this to tell Mama that I love her! I have on many occasions, since I dropped my body, taken her right thumb and tapped it three times saying I love you. She *always* knows it's me. The number three is an important part of the code language that we use since I transcended.

All Spirit Beings use numbers to communicate, and many people are aware of this. Just like individual letters, numbers have energetic signatures that are heard and *felt*. These are unique to each letter and number since each is carried on a specific frequency. This is so for numbers zero through nine. Beyond nine, the frequencies become more expansive, and when letters are combined to make words, the frequencies become more complex. Then, when words are put together in sentences, the complexity increases even more.

When using numbers to communicate, the way it works is similar to the symbolism used in dreams. Each person on both sides of the communication using numbers—the one expressing and the one receiving—creates the meaning of each unique message delivered when a certain number or number combination is shown. I use the numbers three, nine, and twenty-three to send messages to my Mama every day. Most days she receives them loud and clear whenever she sees one of these numbers.

The number twenty-three is my most important number to use to send messages, and within a few weeks of my leaving, my Madre noticed this number showing up everywhere. I used it like a beacon of light to get her attention because it was so important to do so. She has been writing down all the times I show her the number twenty-three since I left and has been on a quest to discover the deepest meaning and messages I share with her about this number. She's far along the path but has yet to know all there is to know. When she's completely ready to know, she will be shown.

This knowing is an odyssey for her and has been like putting together a jigsaw puzzle. She's being given the pieces a few at a time. Each time I show her number twenty-three, it's another piece of the puzzle. Sometimes she sees where it fits, and sometimes she puts it on the side, knowing she will find its spot later. Watching this process unfold from my side brings me great joy! When I was in physical form, I enjoyed watching my Madre do jigsaw puzzles every year at Christmastime. I couldn't actively participate in putting pieces into the puzzle then, but I can now!

One of the first times I used the number twenty-three to get her attention was shortly after I transcended. She was staying at our condo in downtown Ft. Worth that was on the twenty-ninth floor, and one day she was in the elevator on her way up when I stopped it on the twenty-third floor. She noticed the floor number when the doors opened, and she thought it was odd that no one was on that floor waiting for the elevator. Then she continued to floor twenty-nine. She started to wonder why the elevator had stopped on twenty-three. My sister, Alexis, was coming to visit her that day and when she arrived, the first thing she said when she came in the door was that the elevator had stopped on floor twenty-three when she came up!

My Madre became quite curious and began her quest. She soon became fascinated because she realized I had lived twenty-three years, and I had been ill before dropping my body for twenty-three days. I had been created on her birthday, which is March 23. Once I had her attention, I was able to lead her into many fascinating discoveries using this number.

I guided her to purchase "The Book of Stones" by Robert Simmons so she could deepen her connection to earth and nature. Learning about the vibrational frequency of the stones on GAIA was necessary to help her tune in to the "channel" where I could reach her often. She had learned about angels, numerology, cosmology, and spirituality. It was time for her to learn about the communication power within stones.

The day the book arrived, I had her close her eyes and allow me to open it for her. The stone on the page it opened to was Auralite 23. She had never heard of this stone—but I knew of it! As she read the information about this unique, beautiful stone, she knew she needed to get it in her hand as soon as possible. The energy of this stone carries the violet ray of spiritual light to GAIA, and it stimulates higher awareness and telepathic connection to one's Spirits, Guides, and Guards. One of its many unique gifts is that it offers a direct and immediate link to the magic presence in the higher realms—realm twenty-three—where I am now. It also enhances the capacity for Spirit Soul travel and experiences with Spirit beings. So, her Auralite 23 became a powerful tool for us to use to connect and communicate right away. She has also shared this stone with many others who want to feel my energy close to them, and she always keeps her "Spencer stone," as she calls it, nearby.

I continue to use the number twenty-three in multiple ways to send Madre magical messages nearly every day. Sometimes, I'll flash the number just to say hello, I'm still here with you *always* and *in all ways*. Anytime she sees the number, she gives her attention to watch and listen for my incoming message. Other times I use twenty-three to mark a significant time or event to remind her that I'm actively involved in her life cocreating with her, so she knows she's never alone.

One such occasion was when our home at 329 Country Court sold, and the closing date was set for November 23. Of course, she knew I chose that date, so she had nothing to worry about because it was all part of the grand plan!

Another time the number had profound significance was when we set out on our adventure driving to Belize in the Spencermobile. It was intended that we left on February 23, and that was a day that marked the beginning of the end of more than one cycle in both our lives.

I recently guided her awareness to a hidden complex use of the number twenty-three that was "coded" into one of Jason Aldean's songs that I would make her play repeatedly. The song is "1994," and although there's only a few lines in the song that were messages, they're deeply relevant.

Jason sings, "Hop on my rocket ship and let's get outta here, put a little shimmer in your atmosphere. Let's get outta this town and take a few tick-tocks off of your clock" (which happens when we astral travel).

When I dropped my body while entering the True Light with Shima, I was in an MRI machine at Baylor Hospital. Madre was behind the glass window with Dad, the medical staff, and technicians running the tests. The moment she went into that room, she turned around, looked at me in that machine, and "saw me (my Spirit Soul) in a rocket ship" in a fleeting glance. In that instant she knew I had left even though it wasn't confirmed until a little later. Just a few months ago, she was listening to our Jason playlist and this song began to play. I told her to notice that the numbers, from the song title "1994" are 1+9+9+4, which equal twenty-three! This is an example of how coded telepathic messages are delivered.

Last night, I reminded her of the time I showed her the number twenty-three, when she was deciding what to do with my collection of fire trucks, which included an ambulance with paramedics and a stretcher with a person on it. She decided to give part of the collection to the Argyle Fire Department. Those guys had come to our rescue several times over the years, and I came to know many of them quite well.

They were proud to take the collection and made a spot on their display shelf in their new firehouse. So, when Madre was packing up the ambulance, she remembered all the times we played with those trucks and broke down in a moment of sadness and grief. Then she noticed that the patient on the stretcher was a young boy who was wearing a sports T-shirt with the number 23 on it! She immediately noted the message but didn't know the meaning yet. That puzzle piece lay on the table from 2019 until last night, November 4, 2022, when she realized that it was a coded message of what was to come in my future. I was able to decide how my physical life ended, and one of the decisions I had made was that my last ride was *not* going to be a slow ride in a hearse. It was going to be in an ambulance with my Madre and some amazing paramedics. And it was so.

The vibrational energy of the number twenty-three is that of *grateful connection*. (This is separate from the traditional custom with numerology where the energy of a number with more than one digit is decided by adding the digits together.) The number twenty-three is unique, and its frequency is the wave of joy that leads directly to *the place called love*. Everyone knows connection is important. Connection to each other and connection to all. *Grateful connection* is an energy that resonates at a unique frequency, and when your Spirit Soul experiences the *feeling* of emotions that ride this wave, you find yourself flowing into and out of *the place called love* effortlessly. This place is the reality found in realm twenty-three, and this is where Spirit Souls are home with original Source of all creation.

Another number that I use more often now to send messages to my Madre is nine. As she began typing my words for this section of information, she noticed today's date is November 9! This is how I continually remind her I am with her *always* and *in all ways*. The energy signature of this saying, "*always* and *in all ways*," is the same as the number nine! The energy of this number is extremely important to assist with carrying on. Nine is a powerful number that represents completion of a cycle, which is necessary so a new one can begin. My life in my physical body had to end for my Spirit Soul to evolve.

But my connection to my Madre, my Dad, my sister, Alexis, and many others who hear me now did *not* end. I recently clarified for Madre that she is my scribe as we work together to complete this book to teach others about the gifts discovered when you remember to **Listen to the Silence**. She is capable of teaching others how to do this because she has been preparing for many years. What she has been practicing is remembering that speaking without words is a highly advanced way to communicate. I was the master of this, and she was my student. Now is the time for her to become the teacher. She is doing this as a Freedom Coach & Oracle. Inner wisdom, which is the deep knowing of the Spirit Soul, is another characteristic represented in the number nine. **Listening to the Silence** so that emotions can be heard and *felt* before speaking is key to heartfelt communication. When words are spoken without regard for the emotional energy they carry, harm is often done.

This is important to consider because every word, and every letter of every word, has a vibrational frequency that resonates to carry the sound when spoken. And every letter connects to a number. Nine is the most powerful and unique of numbers. Nine is associated with Sagittarius, which is the zodiac sign I was born under. It is the visionary sign; those born under it tend to seek to serve humanity, like I do, and the energy of the number nine wants to unite all of humanity, as I do. This is the work I continue to do now that I am reunited with my Spirit Soul experiencing the infinite and eternal flow and freedom of joy *always* and *in all ways*. This is the work of "The Jasons," and I am an aspect of that collective of Watchers. Nine has the highest vibrational frequency of all the root numbers, and its vibrational energy echoes throughout the cosmos infinitely and eternally. This means its universal quality always shines through.

I started using the number nine to send messages to Madre about a year after using twenty-three. It didn't take her long to notice I was using another number to expand our conversations into a deeper and broader realm. However, it took her a little while to know that when one number code wasn't present, the other was to offer her guidance when she was facing important choice points in her life. I initially drew her attention to the number nine using the help of my good friend Jason Aldean.

When I dropped my body on February 8, 2019, she knew Jason must have been creating his next album, and she was eagerly awaiting its release. She imagined that I would be cocreating with him from my evolved Spirit Soul, and she was curious and excited to listen to his new songs. She knew there would be messages from me coded within the lyrics, song titles, and even the album title. And there surely were!

He released the album on November 8, 2019, which was exactly nine months after I transcended. The day she received notice that it had been released, the first thing she took note of was the title of the album, which was *9.* She downloaded the album, and like always, immediately played it on shuffle so I could play her the song I wanted her to listen to so she would hear my message. That song was titled "Blame It on You."

Only one line in that song was for her: "I *can't* blame it on you." She understood immediately when she heard those words, and I made sure she shared this message with my Dad as well. I wanted them to know that I did not blame them for anything related to my pain and suffering during my last twenty-three days in my physical body. This song was my first opportunity to tell them this clearly.

Mine was not an easy ending for any of us. Our collective suffering was a powerful expression of **grateful connection**. They both stayed by my side throughout every minute of those twenty-three days, and when my Spirit Soul was released from my physical body, many fragments of their Souls remained scattered. I like to use the breath of my whispers of communication to them as breezes softly blowing their Soul fragments back into their *beingness*, with my intentional eternal love for them.

Madre was curious about the album title *9* and knew it was another puzzle piece for her to put aside until she would learn where it fit in the new life she was creating for herself. It takes time to discover the meaning of coded messages—and more importantly, timing must be in alignment for the frequencies to even be accessible. The reverberating echo of the number nine is infinite and eternal, so it continues to circle back around. If it's missed one time, it will return and offer itself again.

Everything has meaning and potential to be revealed when you remember to **Listen to the Silence**.

Potential never ends because it is continuous along the cyclical frequency of the number nine. Have fun with this concept and expand your creativity in joy! All energy in every universe spins, whirls, and twirls in constant motion. Watch the waves in the ocean, the wind as it blows through trees, a dancer or skater spinning on their toes, or a child twirling on a playground. They are all expressions of the frequency of nine. See, hear, and *feel* the joy being shared and know that when you do, you are taking a ride on the wave of joy that leads to *the place called love*.

As each cycle ends, a new one begins. Even after the destructive force of a hurricane or tornado sweeps across GAIA, a new beginning emerges. I use the number nine to guide my Madre now toward her continuation journey, which for now is to remain in her physical body. She follows her own inner wisdom, "inner-standing" well, and when she wants my nod of confirmation, she sees the number nine. When she does, she knows that we are cocreating something wonderful.

Recently, she found herself in Vallarta, Mexico, and she initially thought she was going there to find a place to rent so she could take some time *feeling* the area before deciding to move there. She was only there three days, and on day three she found a place to buy and make a new home for herself. I led her to this new home, and she knew it immediately as she walked inside. My coded messages flashed into her open awareness like neon lights and she "inner-stood" them all!

The community where she now lives is El Tigre. The main gate is "guarded" by two live tigers, and the other gate is called the jaguar gate. She knew I was protecting her here with plenty of *big cat spirit*! Her condo is in the development called Green Bay III (3), and her unit is number 225 (2+2+5=9). Many buildings and structures around the community have owls posted atop corners for the simple purpose of keeping unwanted birds away, but my

Madre knows the greater purpose is owl Spirit watching over her. I reminded her of this the first day she took a restful lay beside the beautiful pool within her neighborhood.

When she looked around at her surroundings, she said in a moment of great joy and gratitude, "I can't believe I'm here!"

I immediately chimed in with *we are here, Madre,* and I shifted her awareness to the top of the building to her far right where an owl is perched watching over her. She laughed and agreed: of course *we* are here, together *always* and *in all ways.*

The address number of both places I lived with my earth family when I was in physical form had the numbers twenty-three and nine coded within them. Our country home was 329 Country Court, and our downtown condo address was 2903 Throckmorton. Both homes were manifested by me and Mama with a knowing that we were meant to live at those places. The energy of both locations was special, and all who visited us *felt* it. Energetic signatures are within everything on GAIA and beyond, and when you remember this, you awaken and activate your potential to expand your spiritual aspect of yourself in every moment you choose to do so. I mastered this when I was there in a body that couldn't move freely about, and I did it without the gift of spoken words. Seek out the highest frequency of energy to enjoy often, and you will find that the key is experiencing—*feeling*—the emotions that are gifted with every thought form shared between you and others who live with you. Be in **grateful connection** to all and **Listen to the Silence**. It will guide you to *the place called love* in realm twenty-three.

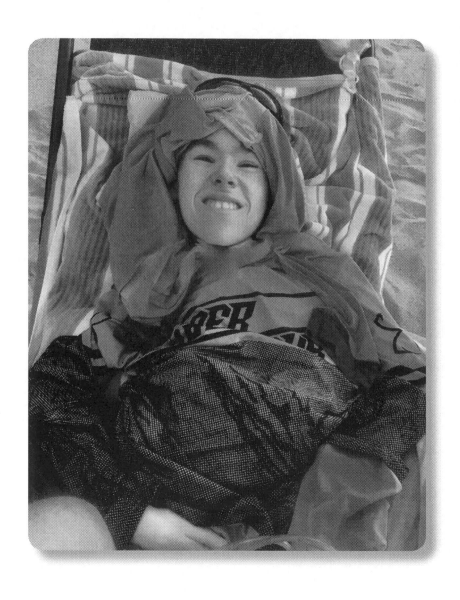

7

SEVEN SILENT YEARS

AFTER I SURVIVED RSV IN 2012, I WAS NO LONGER ABLE TO breathe on my own without the aid of a ventilator, and I had no voice as a result. Although I had lived the first sixteen years of my life without having the ability to speak words, I used my voice to be heard. I expressed my *feelings* with sound so my parents could be in another room a short distance from me on occasion. And I chose to drive my power truck (wheelchair) into a room away from them when I wanted to be alone. In those days, after my hired help went home in the evenings, if my Mama was still working in her office, I would drive myself into my room and look at my photo wall we had created. An entire wall was corkboard, and it was covered with photos of all the things and people I loved with passion. I enjoyed the freedom I had when my body had more abilities, although I never had much independence. I was well cared for and protected. I never had an accident or injury, or illness or pressure sore (bedsore) or dislocated joint or any of the things that are common with people who have physical body issues like mine. I chose my parents well, and they chose all others who were allowed to come into our family circle that was definitely a colorful village.

During my sixty-day battle with RSV, I had a tube down my throat that connected to a ventilator. This was the only way I could breathe because I was not strong enough to activate my diaphragm, and my lungs were heavy with infection. I spent most of my days and nights swimming in the depths of darkness, facing, denying, and taming thousands of beings who dwell there in the underworld, which is *the place called fear.* Many attempted to lure me into their existence with offerings of power in their realm. They were seeking to dim the light of my Spirit Soul that was emitting an "annoying" brightness in their world. Those are the ones I denied. Others were simply making a lot of noise, complaining, shrieking, screaming, howling, or crying out in horror and terror because they had accepted the invitation to remain in the underworld, but they didn't know why. Those were the ones I tamed.

The fever that came along with the RSV was directing the flow of my journey into and out of the underworld. When my temperature spiked, I would be sucked back down into the vortex of darkness that *felt* like the bottom of the ocean within my chest. Since I was in the hospital ICU during this time, and my survival depended on machines and people trained in the field of respiratory functioning to direct my care, we had to abide by their rules. This was extremely difficult for my parents, because they were forced to watch me suffer intense episodes of panic and terror whenever I stopped breathing when the thickness within my lungs had become too heavy for the ventilator to move. The hospital rules only allowed the respiratory therapists to come into my room to suction the mucous out of my lungs and throat "on schedule." My illness was taking my body on its own schedule of needing their help, and these episodes of intense suffering while drowning in my own fluids were grueling.

These were the times I was deep in the underworld, and the light of my Spirit Soul was barely a flicker. My Mama knew when this was so. What she didn't know was that I could see and *feel her* light from where I was, and it is what continued to guide me back. She and I were deeply connected before this time, but once we entered this final chapter of my physical life, our telepathic abilities became much stronger. I had no voice and could make no sound because of the tube that was in my throat. No one could even hear me cough, so my parents learned then that it was necessary to always have eyes on me day and night. They made sure this was so for the rest of my days, and their constant vigilance gave me the confidence and security to stay in my body for seven more years.

During those sixty days in ICU, they never stopped believing that I would eventually emerge from the depth of that illness, and our agreement to continue my life with them was made in *the place called love* in the energy of *grateful connection*. Those seven silent years were an assignment I agreed to take where I would become the master instructor of how to communicate without the use of spoken words *or sound*. I had many students come and go, and when they came into my circle, they attended "class" for minutes, hours, days, weeks, months, or years.

Spencpiration #6

Everyone has an opportunity to remember how to communicate with emotions that envelop every thought form created within the mind when they're in the presence of a silent communicator.

When I agreed to give up my use of expressive sound, I also forfeited my ability to smell and taste. That was in the "fine print" of my addendum to my Soul Contract, and I didn't realize it until several weeks into my recovery. I spent many months *feeling* my anger and disappointment about this but eventually moved past it. Having all these senses removed allowed me to expand and enhance my other ordinary physical senses of sight, hearing, and touch, and my *extraordinary sensory gifts* lit up like a Christmas tree!

I was always sensitive and empathetic toward people, but once I became silent, my ability to *feel* the thoughts of others expanded greatly. When people see someone in a body like mine, they often have thoughts based in the energy of fear, starting with the emotion of pity. I noticed this often during my first sixteen years of life and was always able to quickly convert people's fear-based expression of those emotions by beaming a smile from my pool of joy. However, once I was attached to machines to keep me alive, this task became much more difficult. I could still flash a smile, but my pool of joy had become more of a puddle. My road to recovery was long and it was rough, and my parents and I knew that the only way I would survive was for us to get home.

While we were in ICU, many children dropped their bodies. Whenever this happened, I *felt* the emotions of everyone involved. The medical team of doctors, nurses, and therapists, and the hospital staff of technicians, social workers, chaplains, and aides all did the jobs well that they were trained to do, but the emotions that they were trained to *not feel* couldn't hide from me.

I was also keenly aware of the other children who were suffering illnesses because many were also separated from their physical bodies in that place that's "neither here or there," in between worlds where I was. This is so at every hospital, and many Spirit Souls become trapped in that place. I was especially aware of the other parents who were connected to their children and doing their best to be strong for them, like my parents were for me. Every time a crisis came in the ICU, the flood of fear spread throughout all the rooms, and I always knew when it reached my parents. I heard their thoughts screaming *no, no, no! This is not going to happen to us! We are going to get Spencer out of here* alive.

It was during this time that we made a silent pact. My Mama, my Dad, and I agreed that this hospital was not going to be where my life would end. We decided that once we got out of here, we would not go back into that environment when it was time for me to leave. And that was my choice made in complete silent agreement. My parents **Listened to the Silence** and my ending was of my own creation seven years later.

During those seven years, there were a few times when I was in crisis, and we needed to "review the agreement" because in those moments of panic, it was never easy for my parents to watch me stop breathing and resist the temptation to dial 911. I knew this was hard for them, but whenever it happened, I always sent them encouraging messages of my confidence in their ability to get me through. This deepened their knowledge and our connection throughout those years, and I kept breathing because of that *grateful connection* with them and to many others who came into my life during my final years.

The sounds made by the ventilator became my "voice" in many ways. I learned how to use it to communicate. My Mama tuned into its expressions of my breath moving in and out. Whenever I coughed, it made a distinct clicking noise. She could be anywhere in our house and would come to me when she heard this, day or night. She knew it meant I was in crisis and whether the person assigned to be with me at that time noticed or not, Mama was my *chief rescue officer.* All the machines that were prescribed for me to use when I became labeled as "failure to thrive" were annoying with all the noise they made, and their alarms were disruptive to our peace.

Once we got home, we started the process of removing each of them from use because we came to realize the machines that were assigned to watch over me were a poor substitute for genuine human connection. The best medical professionals know this truth. Always look at the patient first before the machines. The importance of this was demonstrated clearly at the time of my final departure.

The first machine that we eliminated when I got home was the oxygen concentrator. This machine and all its tubes along with the oxygen tanks were placed in a closet and never used because they were not needed. My oxygen saturation was measured by another machine that annoyed me because the numbers were not as important as some wanted to believe they were. Mama and I wanted to be rid of it right away, but we were coerced into using it for the first year, but only at night. However, one night it would not stop alarming no matter what Mama did to silence it, including unplugging it, so she took it outside and threw it off the balcony! My Dad found it the next morning and knew it was never coming back into my room.

Another machine they insisted I needed was a heater and moisturizer for the air coming into me from the ventilator. That machine malfunctioned numerous times, and when it did, the air coming into me *felt* like I was breathing ice cold wet air—because I was! Since I had no way of using words or sound to tell anyone this, I found a way to let my Mama know I was *feeling* cold by breathing out several short breaths, which she heard through the ventilator. When she *felt* the tubing coming from that machine and then *felt* my neck, she *felt* how cold the air was and knew it was miserable for me.

To figure all these things out, my people learned to **Listen to the Silence,** and I learned to sharpen my silent communication skills. The pathways that are available for us are firmly connected to the heart. The heart is where they're to be processed. When thoughts are wrapped in the molecular envelope of an emotion *felt* within the heart, the spiritual messengers—emotions—deliver those messages with clarity and inner knowing.

Emotions are gifts, and my condition evoked plenty of emotions in everyone who crossed my path. I learned to use them to express myself without the use of sound to carry them to others. I could create a thought that released a spark of light, wrap it in an emotion that was a specific frequency, and send it out without the wave of sound. Of course, I engaged the assistance of many of my "winged friends" who are Spirits, Guides, and Guards. The people

I interacted with learned to open their emotional receptor sites to receive my messages without the need for spoken words or sound.

Seven years in silence is a long time to experience this in the 3D realm because there is so much mental chatter and spoken noise that is constantly shared among people. Very few of you realize how important it is to spend some time in silence both alone and with each other. Whenever someone was assigned to watch over me during the day, it was rare that they could sit by my side and not talk. They all were taught how to communicate with me, as that was a requirement to be allowed in our village. I was able to clearly express "yes," "no," and "maybe" and would do so when I was asked a question in the form that could be answered with one of those three choices. To answer yes, I would clack my teeth together once. I said no by shaking my head side to side, and to say maybe, I moved my eyes up and then back and forth.

This meant that those asking the questions must learn to put all communication in the form of a simple question. That was the hard part for people to learn because it required patience and thoughtfulness before speaking. Once they mastered this simple system, we could converse all day without needing one of my parents to translate.

As I said, most people who were assigned to sit by my side talked to me a lot, as if I was their therapist or priest there to hear their confessions. I was a good listener and people do need to be heard. I offered my heartfelt support to anyone who needed to be heard, and I always knew when someone was hurting because I could *feel* their emotional pain the moment they walked into my room.

As soon as they said hello to me, I'd lift my chin to them, which meant, "What's up?"

I could get anyone to tell me everything going on with them if my Mama was in the other room! People loved to tell me their "secrets," and they often made the mistake believing that those secrets were safe with me.

But they weren't always … like when my sister, Alexis, told me she backed our truck into a pole in the parking lot at a horse show. The moment I saw Mama, I told her about that! Another time, Alexis ran the tractor into the side of the arena wall, and I immediately told on her. My good friend Joe was hunting with me and Dad, and he was shooting at something with his shotgun while standing too close to me, and one of the pellets flew back and hit me in the head. After I got home from that outing I told my Mama that Joe had shot me, but she couldn't get a confession out of anyone until a few weeks later when I was having my cranial sacral therapy session and my occupational therapist, Ms. Joan, found the pellet under the skin on my head and showed my Mama. I told her again then that Joe had shot me, so you can imagine the conversation she had with Dad about that! Another time I ratted out Joe was when we had spent the weekend together, and when I came home, I told Mama that Joe had been smoking weed around me!

I never agreed to keep anyone's secrets, so bedtime with Mama was our time to connect. I could share with her the things she missed while she was working in her office or outside mowing the property. If things came up while she was out there and I really needed her immediately, I could send out an SOS telepathically, and she always came. This surprised whoever was assigned to sit by my side because somehow, they had missed my call for help even though they were physically next to me. This is the power of telepathic communication and *grateful connection*!

Physical boundaries do not exist in the world of energetic thought sharing using frequencies of light packaged within the molecule of an emotion.

My beautiful attendant Amelda was my entertainment for my last years before I moved to Belize. She was always full of joy, fun, and silliness. When she came into our village, she brought her baby boy, Jaxton, with her when he was only a few weeks old. This filled our lives with so much new energy and connection.

I am still in constant communication with Jaxton, who reminds his Mama of this often. Amelda would forget things that were important to me during the day, and I would tell my Mama about it when we were in bed at night. She would forget to turn off my fire trucks after we played with them, and even though I would tell her, she often missed my message. So more than once, after we were settled in bed at night, the fire truck in the other room would sound off, and Mama would have to get out of bed and go turn the truck off.

We decided to create a paper form to "write Amelda up" for her job performance errors. When these things happened, the moment Amelda came into my room the following morning, I looked at my cork wall where her written warning was posted for her to sign. This was all in fun, of course, and we laughed together about lots of things. Amelda was very good at **Listening to the Silence**, and she enjoyed the challenge of knowing what I needed without asking my Mama to translate, and I enjoyed challenging her to improve whenever she missed something.

Whenever someone would say to me, "Don't tell your Mama," they soon found out telling her was the first thing I would do! My aunt Vicki was visiting one time, and she had gone to Sonic for a soft drink. When she was sitting by my side drinking it, I let her know I wanted some, even though soft drinks weren't allowed in my daily meal plan. That made it even more inviting, so Vicki gave me some. The first thing I did was smack my lips with enjoyment. As soon as Mama heard this, she knew immediately what was going on—and Vicki knew she had been thrown under the bus.

Smacking my lips and clacking my teeth together were ways I used to make sound to get attention whenever I needed something. My people were all trained to listen to the signals I sent out to get them to look at me. Once I had their attention, I sent coded messages expressing my wants, desires, and needs.

I could also say many things with my eyes and my eyebrows because I had control over these body parts. My sister, Alexis, taught me to roll my eyes whenever someone annoyed me. I could roll my head from side to side and open and close my lips and teeth. I could move my thumb on my right hand and wiggle my nose.

Those were the only physical body tools I had to use to communicate during my last seven years, and I learned to make use of them. My Mama deciphered all my facial expressions and shared what she learned with everyone else, so I was able to have all my wants, needs, and desires met daily. Every itch was scratched; my choice of TV shows was known; I was covered up when I was cold; I received suction when I needed it; my body was shifted when I was uncomfortable; I was rubbed and massaged when I had a pain; and I even directed the activity in the kitchen when my meals were being blasted and my homemade pasta noodles were to be cut.

All of this was possible because my people cared enough to **Listen to the Silence**. My eyes were my greatest tool, and my ordinary physical sense of sight became sharper when I forfeited my senses of taste, smell, and expressive sound. For me to be able to engage someone in telepathic conversation, once I had them look into my eyes, a connection was established. I could create a thought using light frequency, wrap it in the molecule of an emotion, and deliver it quickly and efficiently without the use of sound waves. This was very simple to accomplish when people were not distracted with noise pollution inside their own minds and within our shared space.

I enjoyed many hours with my people outside in nature where we all could **Listen to the Silence** together. We would gather on our back patio by the pool under the shade of a huge oak tree during the day for many hours with family and friends. Or at night beside a fire in the chiminea while star gazing and moon gazing. I had many opportunities with my Dad and our friends camping in our Thor motorhome sitting by a fire at night, riding around the ranch in "La Machine" or our HuntV, or going out on a boat on a lake or the ocean during the day. I spent months with my Mama sitting on the beach by the Caribbean watching pelicans dive for fish during the day. The beach where we lived offered spectacular moonrises over the water and sunrises as well. We watched every moonrise during the six months we lived there. We also spent time by beautiful rivers in the jungle listening to the howler monkeys and watching for jaguars. These moments in nature are when my greatest memories were created during my twenty-three years in my earth suit as Spencer.

These were the times I was able to teach my people how to **Listen to the Silence**. During these times, there was much less focus on doing and more on being. I was *gratefully connected* to all the people who spent time sitting by my side for hours, days, weeks, months, and years. They all were in service to me in my time of need, and I constantly sent out frequencies of radiant gratitude to them. I know they felt this.

Gratitude is an emotion that rides a very high vibrational frequency. It rises above the denser emotions that were evoked when I needed something to relieve my pain, discomfort, or suffering. I infused the shared space with my gratitude to create harmony as my gift to those who were in service to me. I know this was received because when it is so, it raises the entire experience in an upward vortex, always moving toward *the place called love*, which is where all Spirit Souls exist in the flow of the eternal and infinite nature of original Source energy.

I'll see you when I see you, here in realm twenty-three—and I hope it's real soon!

8

THE JASONS

Everyone who knew me as Spencer knew how much I loved Jason Aldean. I could listen to his music all day every day and never get tired of hearing it. What everyone did not know was that my connection to him went much deeper than the physical level of love for his music.

The name Jason means *healer*. Much of what I am going to tell you will not be accepted by some reading my book, and that's okay. The knowledge will be available to you when your Spirit Soul is ready to know it. For now, what most everyone does know is that names have deep meaning. Some people realize this and research names before their children are born, thinking they are solely deciding a name for them. But the truth is, every Spirit Soul chooses their own name when agreeing to come into an earth suit for another round of human experience. The energy of a name is coded into that agreement, as is the time and date of your entrance into physicality (your earth birthday), and the parental humans providing the DNA that will share the experience with you. All letters, words, and numbers are associated with a unique vibrational frequency of light and sound. Sound is light slowed down. All these waves of light and sound blend together uniquely to create you at the moment of inception.

Waves of frequency carry these energies into existence and are an integral part of who every human is. Some people realize during their lifetime that the name they're using is not of their own choosing, and they eventually discover their Spirit Soul's true name along their path of personal expansion. Some do this and choose to change their name to what they *feel* aligned with, while others keep multiple experiences running simultaneously using different names.

My sister, Alexis, expressed this phenomenon when she was young. She was great at acknowledging several different *parallel personas* that were all playing out within her existence, and she shared this freely with our Mama, who always played along. Alexis would wake up and announce that her name was Grace, or Dyan, or Ginger, or something other than Alexis. She would be in the character of whatever name she chose for a few days or sometimes weeks. Her spiritual path will guide her back to where she can discover the deeper meaning of those times in her life, and she will connect to each of them when she is ready to remember to have fun with that!

My deeper connection to the name Jason was being shown to my Mama in pieces, along with the numbers twenty-three and nine. During my final twenty-three days in my physical body, the shape of my face changed drastically. It became very round and swollen because of the activation of the molecule that infected my body and ended my life. I had an autographed photo of Jason Aldean on my corkboard in my room, and my Mama kept looking at my face and comparing it to that photo of Jason. This wasn't a literal transformation that was happening but was visually symbolic, and the coded message within was received by her. It was the same as when I showed her what my face would look like once I had dropped my body. I was showing her *me as Jason*. We were all delirious from more than twenty days and nights without sleep by the time this was happening, and my Mama was very confused, but she had the knowing that it had meaning. This puzzle piece was put to the side for her to find its place later.

Later came on the day I showed up to visit her for the first time as "The Jasons." Mama was in her kitchen at her townhouse at Eagle Circle one morning in 2021 having her coffee and deciding what music to play so she could enjoy her morning meditation. She sensed a Spirit presence that she hadn't known before and thought it was me, but she also *felt* something different. She heard, "Play Jason Aldean music," so of course her first thought was that it was me—as Spencer! Who else would suggest listening to Jason Aldean music to meditate?

But she also sensed a grander presence, so she asked, "Who are *you?*"

We answered, "Jason," and she laughed and said, "Of course you're Jason, Spencer!" (She and others had been referring to me as "Spencer Jason" since I dropped my body and used Jason Aldean songs to send them messages so often.)

Then I said to her, "No, Madre, I am **The Jasons,**" and told her to look up the meaning of the name Jason. She immediately did, and that's when she learned that the name Jason means *healer*. In that moment we told her that we are here to assist with the healing of humanity.

This was a "mic drop moment," and Madre spent the next days, weeks, and months on a path of expansive discovery. She has learned a great amount of knowledge and still has much more to know. The Jasons is a collective of Watchers, and we are empowered with great capabilities, enabling us to freely traverse all worlds. We have deep compassion for humanity and great respect for the human experience. It is a complex adventure, and from our view of this world on GAIA, there is great potential that is prevailing as it finds its way to the frequencies of joy, connection, passion, peace, harmony, and all those emotions that lead to **the place called love.** This is where we exist—when we're not everywhere else—and we're connected *always* and *in all ways* to the original Source of *all*. We are capable of having multiple experiences because we remember the true essence of who we are, and our connection to this is what secures us to the original Source that we always return home to. The unity of *divine feminine and sacred masculine is original Source,* and this union is within every being in every form ever created. Remembering this about yourself is your key to come and go to and from **the place called love** freely.

It is our role as Watchers to guide you on to the brilliant path that leads you home. Home is where you return to recharge so you can continue to expand your Spirit Soul infinitely and eternally. **The place called love** is not a destination; rather, it is a retreat experience where reorganization and integration can occur. The Spirit Soul always knows when it is in **the place called love** because all emotions are *felt* in their ecstatic, expanded, flowing way since there is no construct of judgment here. Watchers keep watch over the entire cosmos, including but not limited to GAIA. The Jasons are a collective whose focus is on humanity, so we watch over you *always* and *in all ways*. We communicate with you in many ways, including shape shifting, and using song lyrics or song titles, orbs, and the bright lights that shine in your night sky.

I told Madre to go to the beach in Puerto Morelos one clear night in June 2022 so that I could send her a message. My instructions were very specific, and she followed them perfectly. I told her to look up at the stars for a sky miracle to appear, and she did. I called her attention to the sky over the ocean and told her to look for a black panther in the stars. I knew she would see it clearly, and she did. The right eye of this panther is the star Arcturus, and the left eye is Spica (from my side). There is a third star that represents the nose and mouth of the face of a panther. I let her know that I am always watching over her from beyond the cosmos, and she finds me in the night sky everywhere she goes since I revealed this to her. Arcturus has a red-gold glow and is known as "the bear watcher," but my Madre knows it as the eye of a black panther!

I agreed to accept the original assignment to have the human experience as Spencer Gray. Watchers can experience life from any form they choose, and they do so often. The Jasons choose to experience life in human form for the purpose of assisting humanity by becoming fully immersed in physicality on GAIA, often in exceptional form, as I did. My original Soul Contract was an agreement to live for sixteen years in a body that could not move itself independently and could not speak words. My date of birth into that body was December 7, 1995. The energy of that was the number seven, and the energy of sixteen years is also the number seven. When I signed the addendum to my Soul Contract and agreed to stay another seven years, that was an upgrade. The opportunity for me to continue more deeply immersed in the human experience in a body that became completely dependent on the connection to other people in total silence was offered to me, and I accepted. The greatest challenge within this experience was to find ways to vibrate in the higher frequencies of gratitude, happiness, acceptance, curiosity, connection, exploration, surprise, amazement, and laughter. The determination to seek these emotions and activate them by *feeling* them was instrumental to my success with my final seven-year mission.

This was accomplished in cooperation with my Madre and my Dad because they were cosigners on this seven-year agreement. We worked together as a team and the task was daunting. Expanding the village was necessary for my needs to be met, and this was not an easy variable for my family to manage. We were all impacted with growing pains as the walls of privacy that protected our family circle were torn down during the invasion of institutions within the medical profession who wanted to take dominion over my care. They had not met my Madre and had no idea how formidable she was, especially when it came to knowing what was best for me. Her ability to unite with me by **Listening**

to the Silence as I communicated my own desires to her was always prioritized.

This was demonstrated in many ways throughout this seven-year journey. For example, all the paperwork the institutions presented were signed by me personally, not by my parents for me. I was always respected and empowered to do this. Each agent who would do their job to read over agreements for services, equipment, and supplies to be delivered for our use was instructed to direct their questions to me personally. They were shown how to put all questions in the form of those that I could answer with my clear yes or no. Once I agreed with a yes, my Madre put the pen in my hand with hers over mine and assisted me in signing my own name to these documents. This is *grateful connection,* and our union and deep commitment to each other was solid throughout the entire assignment.

As the years passed, the dynamics within our home were under constant high pressure. My parents did not sleep restfully for seven years. They both continued to work their jobs during the day and spent every night in bed with me. We all spent nights in the same room for six of the seven years, and during the last year, they took turns going to another room for some hours of rest away from the noise of the ventilator and suction machine and my constant need for suction and adjustment in bed all night. They watched over me continuously and now realize that The Jasons were watching over all of us.

The Jasons were there in many forms, day and night. When I was tucked into bed at night, I was surrounded by strategically placed Spirit animals who were all Watchers on assignment by my side and at my head. Our bed was crowded, but each of these stuffed animals had an assignment as part of my team of protection. There was a giant bear that slept at my head along with a white horse, and a large black panther that was posted as sentry in my window. A jaguar caressed my neck, and a baby tiger was used to prop up my ventilator tubing so that it didn't pull on my trach tube during the night. This kept me from ever having irritation around my stoma, which would have led to infection. Our bedtime routine was a ceremony and The Jasons were there *always* and *in all ways* watching over me and my parents, who never left their post during those seven years. We were **gratefully connected,** and I was able to express my gratitude to them when they would take my hand into theirs and I would tap my thumb three times, saying I love you to them.

The Jasons came in full force as Watchers when I was in ICU for sixty days in 2012. They were my constant protective companion in many forms and always accompanied me into the depths of the underworld. I was able to deny and tame the dark energies I encountered there because I was assisted by the army of Watchers who knew how to support me during these explorations. Their role in this capacity is to guard, and they wielded powerful weapons of energetic light force to strengthen my own protective armor when I needed this reinforcement. They provided the spark that ignited my fire and turned it into a flame blower when necessary. This is how I denied the dark energies that attempted to lure me into their part of the underworld.

The Jasons took the form of a crimson dragon that I rode upon whenever I was descending to these deepest depths when my fever spiked. They also offered me a softer assistance by taking the form of a blue-violet dragon that I rode upon whenever I was ascending from the deepest darkness of my waves of fever with RSV. During these times I encountered those energies who could be tamed and set free. We were able to rescue many who had the desire to ascend the depths of the underworld by offering them an opportunity to connect magnetically to the receptive force of light that was rising like an elevator every time my fever receded.

My ability to rescue Spirit Souls from the other worlds that surround all hospitals did not end when I left the hospital in 2012. I had learned the cosmic guidelines for safely "picking up hitchhikers" while I was immersed in the waves of the underworld during those sixty days in ICU.

Rule number one: only offer a ride to those who ask whenever on the ascension path riding a blue-violet dragon, but never when descending while riding a crimson dragon. My process of transcendence was a twenty-three-day event, and my final twenty-three hours were spent in a hospital.

Even though we had agreed that we would not go back to that setting for my end, I made this choice for several reasons. One of those reasons involved my desire to be in a place where I could offer some lingering Spirit Souls a ride when I made my final ascent. I knew my blue-violet dragon could carry some extra energies, and many of them had been lost in this otherworld for long enough. They connected magnetically to our receptive force of light, and we took them along.

This is an important task for The Jasons to perform and for all humans to know about. So many are programmed to believe falsehoods about the process of transcendence, and they get trapped within this otherworld as a result. They just can't find the True Light that leads to *the place called love*. The tricky tricksters are always busy planting programs and running programs that lead people into these traps. Where they end up is *the place called fear*.

I recently took the opportunity to teach my Madre about my rescue mission, and although it was a painful one for her to experience, she found its meaning quickly because she **Listened to the Silence**. The hospital where I dropped my body is in Grapevine, Texas, which is where she moved to after selling our home at 329 Country Court. Whenever she drove anywhere in the area, she took any route she could find to avoid going past that hospital. If she couldn't avoid it completely, she intentionally looked away as she drove past because her memory of our final moments there were too painful for her to endure. One night a few months ago, she was driving home and found herself in the wrong lane when she approached the intersection where she always bypassed the hospital. The lane she was in took her directly past the entrance to the parking lot, and she couldn't do anything to avoid it. She began crying and calling out to me, asking how I could do this to her. Then she pulled the car into the parking lot and sat there staring at the sky above the hospital.

That's when I told her that if she would see this location as my beautiful place of ascension, she would no longer feel pain. And that's when I told her that I also took many more with me as I left February 8, 2019.

Spencpiration #6

When you be who you came here to be BEFORE you do what you came here to do, you will have all you want in life.

9

ENDINGS MATTER

ALL ENDINGS ARE IMPORTANT. THE END OF SOMETHING IS WHAT people remember, especially when you consider that everything is a relationship. The emotional aspect of relationships is what binds the memory of experiences to your Spirit Soul and within your heart. Take care to honor endings, and you'll be able to see them as the building of bridges that lead to new beginnings.

I loved to watch my Mama wrap presents at Christmas. She spent time with every step of her process that started with finding the perfect box, putting the item inside, taping it, choosing the gift wrap, measuring, cutting, folding, and taping the paper with precision. Next, she would wrap it in ribbon in different creative ways, find the perfect bow, and then make a name tag for the gift using a small piece of the same paper she used to wrap it. That was the finishing touch or ending she put on every gift with great care. After gifts were wrapped, she loaded them into my trailer that I pulled behind my power truck (wheelchair), and I would drive them into the living room where our fourteen-foot majestic Christmas tree stood in the center of our home. I was her helper elf, wearing my jingle bell antlers, who got to decide where each gift was placed under the tree. This shared experience brought me so much joy every year.

My Mama showed the same care to my body when my life had ended as she did every gift she ever wrapped to go under the Christmas tree. After my Spirit Soul left and the machines were turned off, she removed all the tubes, needles, sensors, and tape from my body because they were no longer needed. Once I was free from all the cords, tubes, and physical attachments, she picked me up and took me to a chair in the room where we sat together with my head lying on her left breast. She wanted to hold me in her arms, hug and kiss me one last time, even though she knew I wasn't "in there" anymore. It was her way of honoring the garment that was woven with my Spirit Soul for twenty-three years.

When she was finished holding me, she took me back to the bed and put my body on my side facing the window like she did every night at bedtime. She lovingly placed a pillow between my legs, because this was always done to prevent pressure sores. She swept her hand under my ear to make sure it wasn't folded because that too was always done for my comfort. She positioned my head just so, like always, so I looked like I was resting peacefully. Then she covered me up, tucked me in, kissed me on the cheek, and left my body there. The symbolic gift tag she wrote said, "To original Source. From Spencer's Earth Mama." I shared her heartfelt gratitude for that part of our incredible journey that ended when life in my body did.

She honored my body that was merged with my Spirit Soul for so many more years than most people thought was possible. I created multiple miracles in partnership with that body, but when my end time arrived, both she and my Dad knew it immediately. The molecule that was activated in January 2019 began its job of ending my physical life. I was away with my Dad on our final trip together, and he sensed that something serious was going on in my body because all the things he knew to do to ease my symptoms failed. He called my Mama and tried to describe what he was observing as best as he could.

She knew in that instant that the "beginning of my end" had started. We all three knew. My Dad loaded our things and cut our trip short because he knew we needed to get home, and he knew I needed to be in the presence of my Mama. The moment he carried me into my room, she knew without any doubt that my transcendence process had begun. There was no optimism felt as before with prior events of struggle or suffering. This event was the one and only time that she could not figure out what to do to keep me alive.

During my final twenty-three days, I endured severe pain in my neck and head as the molecule of destruction created infection within my body. The infection was creeping throughout every system within me, slowly destroying my cells of light and life. Of course, the target easiest to attack was my respiratory system, and fortunately, my parents knew how to use all my equipment to offer me as much relief as was possible during this time. They never left my side, day or night. They kept me as comfortable as they could and managed my end-of-life care beautifully—much better than any hospital institution ever could have.

The most difficult part, even harder than my own pain and suffering, was watching their despair, helplessness, grief, sorrow, and feeling of defeat. The amazing fortitude they maintained during those twenty-three days provided the strength that carried me through every confrontation I encountered within the depths of the underworld, which is where I was most of the time. The crimson dragon was my steed as before, and we found ourselves in the heaviest darkness of pain-filled suffering imaginable. There are dark forces there that are remnants of miserable Spirit Souls. They wanted to be heard, and my essence of light and love beaming from my Spirit Soul was noticed by them. I could not rescue them as before when I journeyed there in 2012. This time, there was no blue-violet dragon offering me a lift because there were no waves of descending and ascending with this experience. Only descending into deeper and darker areas because this time, I was not returning to physical life.

However, I did find the True Light on the *other side of the darkness* because I endured my way through it and trusted my crimson dragon, who was The Jasons, to guide and carry me.

What I was able to offer the miserable Spirit Souls I met was a tiny piece of my own light from my Spirit Soul to use as they chose. This is all we can ever do to assist others we encounter along the path of their own journey toward ascension whether in the underworld, in human form on GAIA, or in other worlds in the cosmos. All beings are sovereign and must be responsible for their own creations at every choice point along their path. We can choose to see them as evil monsters—or we can see them as the lovable monster character Sulley that was depicted in the silly movie *Monsters, Inc.* There is great power to enjoy when this is remembered. All beings are touched by sparks of love and light when that is shared from another.

My realization that I am **connected freedom**—I am freedom, and I am connected to all—was expanded during the time spent deep in the underworld where darkness is master. The darkness in that place, which is **the place called fear,** can be seen as beautiful, just like the beauty of the night sky that is sprinkled by bright lights shining through the portals you see as stars, planets, and La Luna.

When I had given many sparks of light from my own Spirit Soul to those in **the place called fear,** I knew it was time for me to leave and pass through. I was exhausted physically, mentally, emotionally, and spiritually, and so were my parents. I could see my pathway out of the darkness, and I was granted permission to share some of what was to come next with my Mama. I had entered the final stage of my transcendence process, and my light was very dim and still. She and I were alone together upstairs for some moments, and I asked her to disconnect my ventilator and give me breaths using the Ambu bag.

In that quiet stillness I became untethered from my body.

I was riding slowly on a white horse, and she was riding on a horse next to me, leading mine. I was in my massage chair in our home facing west, and we could see the sun setting through the windows in that room. In that moment I was showing my Mama *her son* disappearing into a new horizon. As we were riding along, people lined the sides of the road, and I nodded left to right as I acknowledged them. They were honoring me and my ascension, and we could both see the entrance to where I was going. It was **the place called love**.

I was so ready to leave at that moment, but it was not quite time for me to go, so I returned to my body for two more days. My parents and my aunt Vicki stayed by my side, constantly supporting me with their immense compassion during these long days and nights. I was in a massage chair that gently rolled me side to side, and I felt like I was floating along on a river that was leading somewhere beautiful. The room was filled with gratitude, and we each traveled to and from **the place called love** continuously. This is the environment every human deserves to experience when they are transcending physical existence, but sadly, it doesn't happen for very many.

While I was in this stage of my journey, my Mama and I were in constant communication because we were together in that place that is neither here nor there. Our thought forms were sparks of light wrapped in emotions, and we sent poetry to each other, sharing our deepest *feelings* that were bathed in the essence of pure, unconditional love. It's important to share words from the heart when endings are nearby.

These were my words to her:

"Dear Mama"
Spencer Lloyd Gray

It's time for me to go now.
   I'll never say goodbye.
   You know my bones are weary,
   And my Spirit is ready to fly.

Death is crawling through my veins;
   I know you see it, smell it, and feel it.
   My breath is barely flowing, and
   You know this is a well-rehearsed script.

I ask you to cradle me softly deep within your Soul,
   And as my light goes dim, do not fan the flame.
   I'll know when to go, so please trust me with this,
   And set me free from this life without a moment of blame.

I'll pass through the veil and leave you behind, but
   You know I'll remain strong in every beat of your heart.
   You and I have spent my whole life in our mystical space,
   Where my silence was heard, and we're never apart.

I'll meet you there often, whenever you call,
   And we'll continue together in love and light.
   So I'll see you when I see you, and I promise you this:
   Your inner light beam will soon return to bright!

My parents sat in silence, one on each side of me throughout
the final hours of my transcendence journey. The minutes, hours,
days, and nights were torture for them. They were my wings my
entire lifetime and were there for me *always* and *in all ways*. Our
relationship is eternal and infinite and is based in the essence of
pure unconditional love. The *feeling* of being **gratefully connected** to

them before, during, and after my physical lifetime is an expression of our Spirit Soul Contract created in **the place called love**.

My Mama wrote these words of poetry during my final hours soon before I went to the hospital:

"Dear Spencer"
Gina Gayle Gray

I gave you life,
And you taught me how to live.
I gave you life,
And you brought meaning to mine.
I gave you life,
And you taught me to forgive.
I gave you life,
And you made me walk the line.

I gave you life,
And you taught me how to love.
I gave you life,
And you helped me learn to fight.
I gave you life,
And you taught me to rise above.
I gave you life,
And you led me to the light.

I gave you life,
And you taught me to be strong.
I gave you life,
And you opened my heart.
I gave you life,
And you taught me to admit when I'm wrong.
I gave you life,
And we will never be apart!

Endings matter, and I was empowered to create and direct my own. The morning of February 7, 2019, my Mama dialed 911 because she knew I wanted her to. My final ride was to be in an ambulance with Mama and the Argyle Fire Department rescue workers who I had honored during my lifetime.

While in the ambulance, the paramedics **Listened to the Silence** and suggested to my Mama that we go to Baylor Hospital in Grapevine. Although I had never been there, they knew Baylor would be the best given the critical condition I was in. We trusted their guidance, and my Dad and aunt Vicki followed along behind the ambulance. I hadn't been to a hospital or a doctor since I had become an adult, so we knew that entering the emergency room was going to be like running a gauntlet. We knew we would be attacked from all sides of the medical institution upon arrival. There were no medical records available, no history of me or any prior hospital visits because I didn't even have a doctor once I reached twenty-one because I never needed one since I was so healthy.

It was clear that the ER staff was full of fear, and we sensed their terror upon seeing me. My parents were completely exhausted from going twenty-two days and nights without sleep, and they knew to be prepared for many questions that were sure to be asked upon my arrival. And they were.

My Mama found her inner strength—and her inner jaguar— and stepped firmly into her intimidating role as *supreme director* of my care. She wore her black boots, and no one dared mess with her when she walked in anywhere in those!

All the diagnostic tests they ran to attempt to discover what infection was coursing through my body failed to deliver an answer. I was a medical mystery my entire life, and my final presentation to the conventional institution, regardless of how prestigious they were, evoked awe and wonder as to how I could possibly be alive. This hospital wasn't given much time with me to try to figure out how to extend my life. I was only in their care for twenty-three hours, and as I said earlier, one reason I had to go back to that environment was so I could show many other Spirit Souls who had been lingering in the worlds surrounding that hospital the way out through the True Light path.

On the morning of February 8, 2019, the doctors ordered a second, more specialized MRI test because they could not believe that all my diagnostic tests had shown my vital systems and organs to be in perfect working order. They could not identify the source of my infection or my pain, and they never would, so their tests were pointless.

I was leaving and was able to create grand miracles in the moments before my final ascent. When I was put into the MRI machine, I was connected to many machines so I could be monitored while the imaging was being done. This process took several minutes, and the entire time I was in the machine, none of the alarms on any of the devices ever made a sound but my life had ended when I was in there. My Mama knew it because when she looked at me from behind the glass, she saw my Spirit Soul leave, although she didn't *know* she knew that—yet.

As I said before, there are things you think you know, things you *feel* you know, and then there are things you *know* you know. My Mama thought she knew, and she *felt* she knew, but she wasn't sure she knew until the testing was completed and she and Dad and the entire hospital staff came into the MRI room.

They moved me from the machine bed and put me back on my own. It was at that time that my Mama was allowed to come to me, and she immediately looked at my face and saw "that face" that I had shown her a few days prior. She began to scream my name and shouted to everyone in the room, who were all busy hooking machines up and going about their work of making sure the monitors and sensors were in place, which was no longer necessary. Then the doctors and staff flew into panicked action and attempted to move her away from me so they could resuscitate me. That's when she shouted at my Dad, who was also in the room, asking if he had received the DNR (do not resuscitate) order. The moment the head doctor heard those letters, everyone was instructed to stand down, and I was returned to my room to be set completely free. The only part of my body that was still functioning strongly was my heart.

It was there that I reconnected with The Jasons, and they guided me to the beautiful Light Being Shima. She is gold and silver light swirled together, and when I saw her, I noticed she was holding my Spirit Soul wrapped in joy. I felt ecstasy as I recognized what she was holding was the aspects of my *true highest self* that are eternal and infinite. Shima is the golden silver electromagnetic light that attracts and collects those fragments of our Spirit Soul that are scattered throughout our lifetimes.

My final words are ones of encouragement to all beings: to live life from your heart and *feel* your way through by allowing emotions, which are messengers, to be heard and *felt*. Live every day **gratefully connected** to others like I did. Today is Thanksgiving Day 2022, and I told my Madre that my book would be completed today, and it is so.

When the time comes for you to leave your physical life, know the difference between the True Light and the false ones that will try to trap you. You will know the difference if you allow your emotions to guide you because you will be able to *feel* your way on to the path to **the place called love**. I'll be here ready to see you when I see you here at my kinda party! With love, *always* and *in all ways*—Spencer, aka The Jasons.

ABOUT THE AUTHORS

SPENCER LLOYD GRAY AND **GINA GAYLE GRAY** ARE SPIRIT Souls who have been together many lifetimes! In their most recent journey together, Spencer was Gina's son. They know each other well, and telepathic communication is easy for them. Spencer lived twenty-three years in a body that never used spoken words to communicate. Gina was his voice since he couldn't speak. The *grateful connection* and unconditional love they shared for each other was *felt* by everyone who met them.

They have written this book to teach others how to have a meaningful relationship with all silent ones who are in physical *and* spiritual form. They want to shine the light on the wisdom that is to be found within the emotions that are shared between silent communicators and those who care enough to **Listen to the Silence.** Emotions are the language of Spirit. Learning to tune in to *feelings* is key to connecting in gratitude and unconditional love.

Spencer and Gina know that the bond between a mother and her child never ends. When Spencer's messages—*"Spencpirations"*— began coming into Gina's awareness soon after he transcended, she knew their wild ride together was continuing with passion and exploration! They sincerely want to teach others how to **Listen to the Silence** to receive messages and miracles that will keep you connected to *your* Spirit beings *always* and *in all ways*.

Printed in the United States
by Baker & Taylor Publisher Services